Editor-in-Chief and Founder:
   Lyndon H. LaRouche, Jr.
Editorial Board: *Lyndon H. LaRouche, Jr. , Helga
   Zepp-LaRouche, Paul Gallagher, Tony Papert,
   Gerald Rose, Dennis Small, Jeffrey Steinberg,
   William Wertz*
Co-Editors: *Paul Gallagher, Tony Papert*
Managing Editor: *Nancy Spannaus*
Technology: *Marsha Freeman*
Books: *Katherine Notley*
Ebooks: *Richard Burden*
Graphics: *Alan Yue*
Photos: *Stuart Lewis*
Circulation Manager: *Stanley Ezrol*

INTELLIGENCE DIRECTORS
Counterintelligence: *Jeffrey Steinberg, Michele
   Steinberg*
Economics: *John Hoefle, Marcia Merry Baker,
   Paul Gallagher*
History: *Anton Chaitkin*
Ibero-America: *Dennis Small*
Russia and Eastern Europe: *Rachel Douglas*
United States: *Debra Freeman*

INTERNATIONAL BUREAUS
Bogotá: *Miriam Redondo*
Berlin: *Rainer Apel*
Copenhagen: *Tom Gillesberg*
Houston: *Harley Schlanger*
Lima: *Sara Madueño*
Melbourne: *Robert Barwick*
Mexico City: *Gerardo Castilleja Chávez*
New Delhi: *Ramtanu Maitra*
Paris: *Christine Bierre*
Stockholm: *Ulf Sandmark*
United Nations, N.Y.C.: *Leni Rubinstein*
Washington, D.C.: *William Jones*
Wiesbaden: *Göran Haglund*

ON THE WEB
e-mail: eirns@larouchepub.com
www.larouchepub.com
www.executiveintelligencereview.com
www.larouchepub.com/eiw
Webmaster: *John Sigerson*
Assistant Webmaster: *George Hollis*
Editor, Arabic-language edition: *Hussein Askary*

EIR (ISSN 0273-6314) *is published weekly
(50 issues), by EIR News Service, Inc.,
P.O. Box 17390, Washington, D.C. 20041-0390.
(703) 777-9451*

European Headquarters: E.I.R. GmbH, Postfach
Bahnstrasse 9a, D-65205, Wiesbaden, Germany
Tel: 49-611-73650
Homepage: http://www.eirna.com
e-mail: eirna@eirna.com
Director: Georg Neudecker

Montreal, Canada: 514-461-1557

Denmark: EIR - Danmark, Sankt Knuds Vej 11,
basement left, DK-1903 Frederiksberg, Denmark.
Tel.: +45 35 43 60 40, Fax: +45 35 43 87 57. e-mail:
eirdk@hotmail.com.

Mexico City: EIR, Sor Juana Inés de la Cruz 242-2
Col. Agricultura C.P. 11360
Delegación M. Hidalgo, México D.F.
Tel. (5525) 5318-2301
eirmexico@gmail.com

Canada Post Publication Sales Agreement
#40683579

Postmaster: Send all address changes to *EIR*, P.O.
Box 17390, Washington, D.C. 20041-0390.

Signed articles in *EIR* represent the views of the
authors, and not necessarily those of the Editorial
Board.

Enact and Implement Glass-Steagall Free the World from The British Monarchy

About This Issue

by Tony Papert

July 14—What is mankind's answer to the problems which threaten the planet at this time? It is self-evident that that question should be the pole-star for the mind of every man and woman, but only a very, very few can even entertain it today. The reason is obvious. Stupidity rules as an iron law over every association in the United States and Western Europe,—except for an occasional one or perhaps two, whose members can be counted on one hand. And the other, equivalent name for stupidity is indifferentism. In the United States, the tyranny is most absolute in the southern states of what is often called the "former" Confederacy, but which is a Confederacy still very much alive, as recent events have underlined.

Indifference to the rights of humanity is intrinsically illegal. No policy may exist which lacks good grounds for existence in those terms. We must cancel Wall Street as having no humanly moral reason to exist: other than money!

At the same time, we must, as the preacher said, "hate the sin, while loving the sinner." Help him face his stupidity and overcome it. Love fights effectively to pull him out of the ocean of stupidity and indifferentism in which he has almost drowned, not to be dragged in after him and join him there. If only the tiniest minority is capable of real intelligence and devotion under current circumstances, that only means that their responsibility is so much the greater.

The test will come. The moment will arise very soon, when "profound and impassioned conceptions respecting man and nature," will be able to permeate much more widely, and work their effects, as Shelley wrote.

Now, from this higher vantage-point, look back to the peak of science attained at the end of the Nineteenth and the very beginning of the Twentieth Century. Einstein, Planck, and Vernadsky saw science as one continuous endeavor with Classical music. Like Beethoven, they consciously crafted mankind's future. Now, the thread of fundamental scientific progress has been dropped, amidst the cultural and scientific degeneracy of the Twentieth and now the Twenty-First Century. What is the next level of science? That is the subject of a LaRouche PAC Scientific Team Research Report in this issue.

Only one week ago, on July 7, the original Constitutional principle of the United States, as crafted by Alexander Hamilton from Manhattan, was placed on the agenda for immediate action by four United States Senators, led by Elizabeth Warren of Massachusetts, who introduced Franklin Roosevelt's Glass-Steagall law for immediate adoption. They did this because they understood that this system, the Wall Street and London-centered financial system of the United States and Western Europe, is finished. Wall Street is about to blow out. The action begun by these four Senators (and 61 U.S. Representatives) must be spread and carried to its conclusion. The nation must return to Hamilton's Principle for its salvation again now, as we have had to do for our survival at every existential crisis in our history.

At the same time, we must denounce and condemn Hamilton's leading opponent Thomas Jefferson, who was always corrupt. Jefferson corrupted the United States from the moment of its founding, on behalf of slavery. The time is long past to end his influence forever.

EIR Contents

www.larouchepub.com Volume 42, Number 28, July 17, 2015

Cover This Week

Alexander Hamilton, Treasury Secretary, 1789-1795.

LPAC

The BRICS New Paradigm Can End Geopolitics

The following is the full text of Helga Zepp-LaRouche's 20-minute interview with Radio Sputnik on July 6, 2015. The interview, which was aired live at 6 pm prime time in Russia, came in the context of an article by Sputnik and Russia Today covering the petition by Zepp-LaRouche's Schiller Institute, which calls for the United States and Europe to dump geopolitics, and join with the BRICS nations.

Estelle Winters, host for Radio Sputnik: Well, to discuss this, I'm now joined live on the line by the founder of the Schiller Institute, the initiator of the petition, Helga Zepp-LaRouche. Thank you very much for joining us here at Radio Sputnik.

May I ask you, first of all, how did you come up with the idea of initiating such a petition?

Helga Zepp-LaRouche: Well, I think first of all, geopolitics was the reason for two world wars in the Twentieth Century; and right now, if it would come to a third world war with thermonuclear weapons, it would lead to the extinction of mankind. So, therefore, the key question is, how can we overcome the thinking of geopolitics by establishing a New Paradigm. A New Paradigm which starts with the common aims of mankind.

The way to look at it is not from the standpoint of present interest of one country or a group of countries, but how can we define the future of humanity. Where do we want to be in 100 years from now? Do we want to be extinct, or do we grow up as a human species? I can tell you that the philosophical basis for this idea comes from a philosopher who is very well known in Russia, by the name of Nikolaus Cusansky (Nicholas of Cusa), who had the idea of thinking on the level of the *Coincidentia Oppositorum*—the coincidence of opposites—which is a method of thinking which very much informed [Russian-Ukrainian scientist] Vladimir

Vernadsky. And Vernadsky called Cusansky the "divine Cusanus," and that is really the idea: that we have to move to a completely different kind of thinking about one humanity. And from that standpoint, try to solve all the conflicts of the here and now.

Winters: Why do you think cooperation with BRICS nations so important for sustainable development of the United States and Europe?

Zepp-LaRouche: Well, the reality is that since the Fortaleza Summit last year in Brazil, the BRICS countries have started to build a completely new system of economics, of economic cooperation. Of a new financial system signified by the AIIB [Asian Infrastructure Investment Bank], the New Development Bank, the Shanghai Cooperation Bank, and similar new financial institutions, which deliberately said "No" to the casino economy of the trans-Atlantic system; and deliberately want to only finance the real economy, infrastructure, and things which are in the common good of the people.

So, given the fact that the trans-Atlantic financial system is completely bankrupt—and that will show in the aftermath of the courageous Greek vote in the referendum—that the trans-Atlantic system is bankrupt and could explode at any moment. Because it's not just the Greek debt which hangs on it, but it's the entire international derivatives market, which amounts to probably around $2 quadrillion. The only solution would be that the trans-Atlantic countries go on the same kind of financial and economic policy as the BRICS, which would be possible if there were a European debt conference, eliminating all the useless, worthless debt of the derivatives. Then go for a global Glass-Steagall separation of the banks in the tradition of Franklin D. Roosevelt.

That was the key measure by which Franklin D. Roosevelt got the United States out of the Depression

EIRNS/Christopher Lewis

Helga Zepp-LaRouche addresses an EIR seminar on the New Silk Road in Frankfurt, Germany on January 29, 2015.

in the '30s. And right now, if the United States would take the leadership in going back to Glass-Steagall—and there are many important people in the Congress, as well as Martin O'Malley, who is a Presidential candidate, who is campaigning for the immediate re-introduction of Glass-Steagall—then there would be a platform for the United States and the European nations to cooperate with the BRICS countries in building the New Silk Road, building the cooperation between the Eurasian Economic Union and the New Silk Road. And that could be the kernel of a new world economic order, which would be in the benefit of all participating nations.

As the Chinese President Xi Jinping has always emphasized, we have to go to a win-win cooperation; this idea of a win-win cooperation is the way to overcome geopolitics. That is the key idea behind this BRICS resolution.

Winters: And tell me about this petition; you're convinced that it will make a difference?

Zepp-LaRouche: Oh yes, because we are using it for international outreach. We are contacting business

leaders, politicians, mayors, city councils, to inform them that the BRICS system is an alternative system of economic cooperation. Because the western media have not really reported objectively about what the policy of the BRICS is. People don't know it, because the only articles which you can read are like "Putin is a dictator," "Xi Jinping is trying to replace American imperialism with Chinese imperialism," and such nonsense. So, people don't have a true idea that the BRICS countries represent a completely new model of political relations among major nations, which is also open to any other nation in the world.

My biggest hope would be, that the BRICS countries issue, at the BRICS summit, some kind of call, an outreach to the rest of the world to join that model. Because I think that something very urgently has to be done to bring the world away from the present brinksmanship policy, which could really go completely wrong, and lead to the extinction of us all.

What we are doing with this petition is to make sure that people know about the BRICS model; that we know there are enormous economic benefits for them, if they would cooperate. It's not just the BRICS countries who need a new economic approach; if you look at the European countries, all of southern Europe is really collapsing as a result of the vicious financial fascism of the Troika.

In the case of Greece, it has destroyed one-third of the real economy, but the situation in Italy, Spain, Portugal is not much better. So these countries urgently need the extension of the New Silk Road, the Eurasian Land-Bridge, into southern Europe to have a real program of reconstruction and economic build-up. The United States is not in such a great condition, either; it urgently needs a transcontinental fast train system, of the type China has been building—China has built 18,000 km of excellent fast trains. The United States would greatly benefit if it would say, "OK, let's go back to an FDR approach," like the New Deal, the Tennessee Valley Authority approach; build infrastructure in their own country. That way we could all join hands and say, "Let's move beyond the danger coming out of geopolitics; and let's join hands to build a future for humanity as a whole."

Winters: Very quickly, were you surprised that

2,000 people signed this petition?

Zepp-LaRouche: No. Actually, I want to qualify that number of 2,000, because I think 500 of them represent very important institutional people; so it's not just single individuals. If you look at the list on the New Paradigm Schiller Institute website, you will find the signers there. And you will see that they are from a very broad range of people internationally who represent extremely important institutions. Then we also have so-called ordinary citizens who are signing it; and they are equally important.

I think what we want to do with this petition is to build an opposition of people who realize that it is much more in their interest to cooperate with Russia, China, India, Brazil, South Africa, than to have a confrontation with NATO against Russia and China. So, I think it would be very good if the listeners of this program would help to spread this resolution; make it known, so it can become a groundswell of people who say, "No, we need a new paradigm," and this is an historical moment in the history of mankind, where we have to absolutely prove that we, as a species, are morally fit to survive. I think the idea of having a just new world economic order is exactly the way to go.

Winters: We all know we're on the eve of another BRICS get-together, this time in Ufa. Do you believe that everybody is aware of this petition?

Zepp-LaRouche: No, I don't think so, but I think your interviewing me is a great help to make it more known; because as I said, this Ufa summit is a fantastic opportunity to not just have, to deal with the internal affairs of the BRICS and then the Shanghai Cooperation Organization countries. But I would really, really wish that it would be used to issue a call to all of humanity in the moment of the greatest danger, to make sort of an evolutionary jump ahead and define the common aims of mankind, and ask other countries to join in this effort. I think if that opportunity would be used, it could be a landmark in getting mankind out of this crisis.

Winters: And you have a representative in Ufa?

Zepp-LaRouche: Unfortunately, not. No, I would like to, but we have not been invited.

Winters: One last thing; what are your future plans to help promote better relations between the West and the BRICS?

Zepp-LaRouche: We are conducting a lot of international conferences. We just had a very important international conference in Paris, of the Schiller Institute, with 500 participants. We have an ongoing series of conferences in New York, in Manhattan, which is based explicitly the idea to get the United States back on its tradition as a republic in the tradition of the Founding Fathers and Alexander Hamilton. We've had conferences in Washington, in San Francisco, in Frankfurt, in Copenhagen; and we will have more such conferences. We would be very happy to conduct such conferences all around the world. Also, if people could join in; because we are doing what we can, but we really need other people to amplify our effort so that this idea of a New Paradigm becomes a common household word.

We have published a report, which is also very important, which is called *The New Silk Road Becomes the World LandBridge*. The Schiller Institute worked out the idea of a Eurasian Land-Bridge 25 years ago, and we already then called it the New Silk Road. We [have] had over the last 25 years, thousands of events—seminars, conferences—promoting the idea of the New Silk Road; and therefore, we were extremely happy when Xi Jinping in 2013 announced the New Silk Road as Chinese policy. I participated just two weeks ago, in a big conference in Yiwu in China on the New Silk Road; and I think it is extremely important that there will be more such conferences.

But for us, the New Silk Road is just a synonym. It's not just the transport connection between A and B, but it's a synonym for the New World Economic Order, and it's not just economics. It must be combined with a cultural Renaissance, because if you look at popular culture in the trans-Atlantic world right now, it is so degenerate, and so Satanic almost—bestial—that we absolutely want to revive Classical culture. German Classical music, Chinese Confucian thinking; in every culture you have some high points, and these have to be revived together. Then you can have a new dialogue of civilization based on the highest level of each culture; and I think that way we can get mankind to a completely new phase in the evolution of civilization.

I don't think we have reached the end of history. If we do what needs to be done now, in this moment, I think we are on the verge of a new golden Renaissance; but we have to mobilize as we have never mobilized before. Because it's an existential moment in history.

Winters: Thank you very much indeed for joining us here at Radio Sputnik. Founder of the Schiller Institute, Helga Zepp-LaRouche.

The Coming Interim Presidency Under Glass-Steagall: The Name of The Future Is Alexander Hamilton

by Robert Ingraham

Adapted from a report given by the author in Manhattan June 6, 2015.

July 12—The anticipated re-enactment of Glass-Steagall legislation in the United States will be the single indispensable action needed to shatter the power of the financial speculators of London and Wall Street, those same speculators who have been leading the United States and the world to ruin. No other transformative act can save the trans-Atlantic economic system, while simultaneously engendering a shift in policy toward a BRICS-like approach to global physical economic development. The July 7 introduction of Senate Bill S. 1709 has now placed that early re-establishment of Glass-Steagall at center stage of the political fight in the United States.

At the same time, the re-enactment of Glass-Steagall will mean an end to the catastrophe of the Obama Presidency and the subsequent emergence of an "interim Presidency" with new policy axioms, which, over the next 16 months, can un-

leash the rapid rebuilding of the American economy together with a transformation of American foreign policy, oriented toward mutually-beneficial cooperation with the BRICS nations. As Lyndon LaRouche declared in a July 10th statement, this will mean a "New Era for Mankind."

The revival of Glass-Steagall is the single most urgent priority facing America. If we act on it now, the world will change, and a pathway out of our current

Alexander Hamilton (right) and Gouverneur Morris (left) were both members of the Constitutional Committee on Style, which put the U.S. Constitution in final form and added the Preamble. Hamilton's portrait was done by John Trumbull in 1806.

crisis will appear. There is no need to panic over the danger of a "financial crash;" Glass-Steagall is the solution.

A successful political battle to re-establish the Glass-Steagall Principle will have a second profoundly important consequence. The adoption of Glass-Steagall will be a revolution against Wall Street, and, thus, a seismic rejection of the axioms of the Obama Presidency. It will signal the end of the Obama Presidency, however that might play out. A new leadership anchored to a Glass-Steagall economic policy outlook will open the door for a revival and re-creation of an actual Constitutional Presidency within the United States.

Alexander Hamilton's economic genius can not be separated from his creation and vision of the American Presidency as the means whereby the future survival, prosperity, and development of the republic might be secured. Glass-Steagall will be an axiomatic revolution in the economic policy axioms of the nation, and its successful implementation will place the issue of the necessary Presidential leadership front-and-center for every American.

The Presidential Principle

Most Americans—let alone foreign observers—have little if any comprehension of what the American Presidency is. Some might define the Presidency as one of "three branches" of our government, with "checks and balances" as they were taught in high school. Others might view the President as a leader, a powerful individual man (or woman), a view which leads to the present day sports-like obsession with Presidential "candidates." A few, very mistaken individuals might equate the office of American President with that of the British Prime Minister or German Chancellor, both of the latter being merely spokesmen for "party-led" or "legislative-led" governments.

A somewhat more sophisticated observer might speak of the "extended-Presidency," i.e. an executive-led leadership which encompasses a broad array of contributing individuals within the nation. That observation gets closer to the truth, but is still not adequate. The problem with all of these descriptions is that they focus on the outer "form" of the Presidential office rather then the content—the purpose—of what the Presidency was designed to be. In truth, the American Presidency is a Principle, a human discovery, a Principle created by Alexander Hamilton, embedded into our Constitution in

1787, and then woven into the very fabric of our nation during the eight-year Presidency of George Washington.

At the Philadelphia Constitutional Convention, in the summer of 1787, Alexander Hamilton, together with his friend and ally Gouverneur Morris, were directly and personally responsible for two great accomplishments. First was the creation of a strong Presidency in the new Constitution; second was the authorship and addition of a Preamble to that same Constitution. There is no possible way to truly grasp the intent behind their creation of the Presidency without putting it in the context of the Constitution's Preamble. That Preamble was neither an "add-on" nor an "introduction" to the Constitution. Beginning with the words "We the People of the United States…," Gouverneur Morris (the Preamble's author) defined both the philosophical outlook and the purpose the new Republic, including the sacred mission to "promote the General Welfare" and to "Secure the Blessings of Liberty for ourselves and our Posterity."

The Preamble demolishes any claim that the American Constitution was some sort of Lockean "social contract," i.e., an agreement among otherwise self-seeking individuals to find a means whereby they could simple co-exist together, free to carry out their individual selfish interests. Rather, the Preamble defines the new Nation as a future-oriented Republic, with a sacred mission towards its citizens, the nation and future generations. The Preamble defines both the philosophy and the mission of the new Nation.

For Hamilton and Morris, the Presidency was the key to this mission. They fought harder on the question of the Presidency than on any other issue at the Convention. In a very real sense the American President is not a "person," per se. The Presidency is intended to embody the Principle embodied in the Constitution's Preamble, to promulgate the Spirit of that Preamble. The Presidency was intended to personify the sacred trust announced in the Preamble and to hold the nation on a path to fulfill its future potential. Thus, the Presidency would lead the Nation.

The Creation of the Presidency

At the Philadelphia Constitutional Convention in 1787 it was the intention of the Virginia delegation[1] to

---

1. Virginia, at that time, being the most populous and politically powerful state. Virginia also contained 50 percent of all the slaves in the United States.

craft a government in which the National Executive would be a mere figurehead, a de-facto puppet of the individual states' interests. The first plan presented at that convention—the Virginia Plan, written by James Madison and presented on May 29, 1787—would have established an Executive Office far weaker than the British position of Prime Minister. Under the Madison proposal the President would be elected by the members of Congress. That Congress, in turn, would function as a mere vehicle for the state governments. United States Senators would be selected by the legislatures of the individual states, and subject to recall if they failed to represent the interests of their states. Members of the House of Representatives would be

The plan for the Constitution drafted by James Madison (above), often touted as the "father" of that document, would have created a Presidency weaker in powers than the British Prime Minister.

elected by the people but only from a pre-selected list of candidates who had been nominated by the same state legislatures. Those state-controlled Senators and Representatives would then select the President from among their own ranks.

Under Madison's Virginia Plan an individual President would be limited to one term, would be subject to impeachment, and would be denied any authority over the armed forces of the United States. All military affairs were to be placed under the control of Congress, and the actual day-to-day functions of the President were largely ceremonial. Under Madison's Plan, the Executive would exist solely to ensure that the will of the legislature was carried out.

On June 13th, a second plan, the New Jersey Plan, was presented to the Convention. If anything, it was worse than the Madison proposal. In the New Jersey Plan a unicameral Congress was to be elected by the individual state legislatures. That Congress would then select the President (again, for only one term) from among themselves, and the President would be subject to removal from office, either by impeachment by the

Congress or by "recall," if a majority of the nation's state governors demanded it. Once more, all control over military affairs was placed in Congress, and the President was to be a puppet of those Congressional (actually, state) interests. The New Jersey Plan essentially created an impotent Federal government entirely controlled by the individual states, with the Office of President mere window-dressing.

Other plans, including the Pinckney Plan and the Connecticut Plan, were also presented to the Convention. All of these various "plans" would have established a toothless figurehead President, elected by, and removable by, the Congress and/or the state governments.

On June 18th George Washington suspended all ongoing business at the convention and turned over the entire day's agenda to Alexander Hamilton. Hamilton spoke for six hours. It is that speech by Hamilton—a speech almost universally derided by historians—which gave birth to the American Presidency. Speaking against the views of a majority of the delegates, Hamilton proposed a Presidency-led National government. Hamilton envisioned a shattering of the power of the individual states and a national Presidency placed unequivocally in the leadership of the nation, including the use of such Presidential authority to determine the future directionality of all foreign and economic policy.

Many of Hamilton's specific proposals—the role of the Executive as the Commander-in-Chief of the armed forces, the power to make treaties and pardon crimes, and the establishment of a popularly elected Electoral College to remove any role of either the state governments or the Congress in selecting the President—eventually made their way into the final Constitution. Several of his other proposals, including a lifetime term for Presidents, the right of an absolute veto, and the appointment of all state governors by the National government, were not adopted. But, putting to one side the various specific details of Hamilton's Plan, it must be recognized that the June 18th speech by Hamilton revolutionized the proceedings of the Convention, placing the nationalists in the ascendancy, and demolishing the idea of either a legislative-led or state-controlled national government.

Gouverneur Morris, practically alone, fought for the direct popular election of the President and against the inclusion of an intermediary Electoral College. In his view this was vital for establishing a "sacred trust" between the President and the People. Morris predicted that in the new government it would become inevitable that Senators and Representatives would tend to serve sectional, state, and even moneyed interests, and it was only in the Presidency that the unified mission of the Nation would have voice. It was the President, and only the President, who would represent the Nation as a whole, and it was the President who would be charged with defending the population and directing the affairs of the Nation toward a better and more fruitful future.

To secure the ability to carry out that mission. Hamilton and Morris fought for the inclusion of broad Presidential powers. Expanding on the powers enumerated by Hamilton in his June 18th speech, Morris, in late July, overturned the previously agreed-upon statute which would have limited the President to one term, thus allowing the re-election of the President without term limits. More importantly, in the final days of the convention, it was the Hamilton-led Committee on Style which changed the wording—and the intent—of what are known as the "Vesting Clauses" in both Article I and Article II, drastically altering the relationship between Congress and the President. In the new wording Congress was limited to "all legislative powers herein granted," i.e., only to those powers specifically enumerated, while the non-specific "Executive Power shall be vested in a President of the United States," established the Principle of the "Implied Powers" of the Presidency.

The Spirit Becomes Flesh

The 1789-1797 administration of George Washington established the model for the functioning of the American Presidency. With Hamilton at his side, and ably supported by Gouverneur Morris, John Jay, and other New Yorkers, Washington demonstrated the power of a President-led government in directing the affairs of the Nation in coherence with the responsibilities defined by the intent of the Constitution's Preamble.

The most striking intervention of the Washington administration was the adoption of the economic philosophy and policies of Treasury Secretary Hamilton. With the drafting of Hamilton's Four Reports, together with the creation of a National Bank and a system of Public Credit, Washington and Hamilton demonstrated that the role of the Presidency, the economic policy of the Nation, and the intent of the Constitution's Preamble were all cut from the same cloth.

During his eight years in office, Washington established a model of Presidential leadership. This included not only the executive "branch," *per se*, but also the appointment of Washington's ally John Jay as Chief Justice of the Supreme Court, the crucial role of both New York Senators, Philip Schuyler and Rufus King, in securing the passage of much of the Washington Administration-authored program through the Congress, particularly their role in the battle for passage of the National Bank legislation. The Washington administration also relied on collaboration with key state government officials, such as Stephen Van Rensselaer of New York and John Marshall of Virginia, and the deployment of a broader array of military and scientific figures. Thus was born the functioning of an "Extended Presidency," which emanated from the Presidential leadership.

Alexander Hamilton's Constitutional economic program, Gouverneur Morris' activities in Europe, other key diplomatic initiatives, the anti-slavery Northwest Ordinance of 1789, and the establishment of the national Judiciary all flowed from the Washington Presidency. Perhaps even more important was the moral and strategic leadership which began with Washington's First Inaugural Address, continued through his annual State of the Union Addresses, his first Declaration of National Thanksgiving and culminated in his 1797 Farewell Address. A current-day re-reading of those utterances paints a vivid portrait of the Presidency as Hamilton and Morris had designed it in 1787.

The Presidency and Glass-Steagall

It is a mistake to think about "the Presidency" and economic programs, such as Glass-Steagall, as separate topics. In the republic crafted by Hamilton, Wash-

George Washington delivering his inaugural address April 1789 at Federal Hall, New York, as depicted by T.H. Matteson, and engraved on steel by H.S. Sadd.

Library of Congress

ington, and their allies between 1787 and 1797, a Constitutional Presidency and economic policies which are both vital to the nation as well as coherent with the creative nature of the human species, are inseparable. Nevertheless, for Hamilton and Morris a Constitutional Presidency was an absolute pre-condition for the future development of the Nation. The Presidency was the key.

For example, Hamilton's National Bank was a profound discovery that made possible the future development of the new Republic. Yet, after Washington left office, that bank never really functioned as an engine for transformative public credit in the manner for which it had been created, except for the brief 1825-1829 years of the Quincy Adams Presidency. Abraham Lincoln and Franklin Roosevelt both accomplished powerful economic revolutions during their administrations, and both did it without a national bank, while the slave-owners Jefferson, Madison, and Monroe all had the benefit of an existing National Bank, but they refused to use its potential powers for the benefit of the Nation. With Lincoln and Roosevelt there existed a functioning Presidency imbued with the mission of the Republic. That is what made the difference.

Neither Hamilton's "Economic Principle," nor the "American Presidency" are "things." They are designed to complement each other and to function as one singular transformative action, with the intention of improving upon the future of the nation and the world. As Hamilton emphasized in his *Report on Manufactures*, the engine for such improvements lies in the rapid scientific, technological, and industrial development of the physical economy. Such an approach will accelerate advances in the productivity, skill levels, and cognitive abilities of the citizenry. Such an approach is also fully coherent with both the current pro-development outlook of the BRICS nations, as well as with the actual creative nature of our species within the galaxy.

A revolutionary re-establishment of Glass-Steagall today will necessitate not simply a change in leadership in the United States, but a change in the species-nature of that leadership. This will have to happen. Neither an Obama nor a Bush is capable of implementing a Glass-Steagall policy. As the failed axioms of speculation and austerity are swept into the dustbin, a revival of a true Constitutional Presidency will begin to emerge. All great changes, all great accomplishments, in American history are associated with a re-awakening, a re-emergence of the American Presidential System.

The American Presidency is both an Idea and an institution which embodies that Idea, which personifies that Idea. As seen in the cases of Washington, Lincoln, and Roosevelt, that executive leadership can stretch out to encompass a broad array of individuals and allies—an "extended Presidency." In a certain sense, that Presidential Idea is embodied in the very notion of an American Citizen.

Senate Glass-Steagall Move Creates A Potential 'New Era for Mankind'

Here is the transcript of the regular Friday LaRouche PAC webcast of July 10, 2015, also available on video.

Matthew Ogden: Good evening, it's July 10th, 2015. My name is Matthew Ogden, and I'm happy to welcome you all to our weekly Friday night broadcast here from larouchepac.com. Joining me in studio tonight is Paul Gallagher from *Executive Intelligence Review*; he is the co-editor, and he's joining me to speak about what has been a very momentous week indeed, and also what the future holds in store. Paul and I had the opportunity to meet with Mr. LaRouche earlier today, in preparation for this broadcast tonight. And the theme that he continued to emphasize was the absolute critical importance of the action that has been taken this week by Senators Elizabeth Warren, Angus King, Maria Cantwell, and John McCain in the United States Senate, to introduce the 21st-Century Glass-Steagall Act, and the urgency of mobilizing behind this action as priority #1.

The bill number of this Senate bill is S.1709, and it's to restore the Glass-Steagall Act. And Senator Warren gave a very passionate speech on the floor of the Senate, announcing its introduction, which I strongly encourage our viewers to watch. This is easy to find on the Internet.

This action by Senator Warren and the three other Senators was also immediately followed the very next day by an open letter that was issued by Presidential candidate Martin O'Malley; an open letter to the Wall Street mega-banks, titled, "Dear Wall Street, I Will Not Let Up on You", in which he also calls, as a central facet of this letter, for the immediate re-instatement of Glass-Steagall. This open letter was also accompanied by a policy white paper that was issued by his campaign, on Glass-Steagall and related measures to protect the American people, and to shut down the criminal activities of Wall Street.

So, this is clearly a coordinated action, and the point that Mr. LaRouche made, both last night and earlier today, about the reason why this decision was made at this precise moment in time; this week, this moment in history, by these four Senators led by Elizabeth Warren, is the subject of the bulk of the remarks that he made earlier today.... We've transcribed a paraphrase of those remarks, and we made them available on the website earlier this afternoon, so maybe you've already gotten a chance to see that. If not, that's available for you to consult as well; but this will inform what we have to say tonight.

What Mr. LaRouche said, is that the members of the Senate who have taken this initiative, should be legitimately recognized and congratulated as heroes. He said that they deserve full credit where credit was due. And he remarked that he was pleasantly surprised to see that there are now leading members of the United States Congress—the Senate in particular—who have finally begun to see reality as he sees it, and have responded. And what is that reality? The question is, why did they decide to take this action at this moment? And Mr. LaRouche said it's because these members of the United States Senate are fully aware that a collapse of the entire United States economy is about to occur if these Glass-Steagall measures are not taken.

Senator Elizabeth Warren presenting the 21st Century Glass-Steagall Act July 7: "The biggest banks continue to threaten our economy. The biggest banks are collectively much larger than they were before the crisis of 2007, and they continue to engage in dangerous practices that could once again crash our economy."

Saving the U.S. and Europe

Why? Because Wall Street is bankrupt, and they know that the entire Wall Street system is in the process of a total collapse. So, as he said, we should congratulate these members of the United States Senate for taking this immediate urgent action. I'm not going to summarize in full what he said, because I know this is something that Paul will address a little bit more in depth. But the point which Mr. LaRouche emphasized is that with this action that's been taken by the Senate, we can initiate, we can begin, what Franklin Roosevelt did in the very beginning of his first term as U.S. President; and liberate ourselves as a nation from these parasites on Wall Street.

And he said with that kind of action, this introduction of the Glass-Steagall measure into the United States Senate this week, portends the greatest recovery action in the recent history of the United States; and in fact, a new era for mankind. And he emphasized that we should call it that, a new era for mankind. He called on the Congress to take its authority to act on an emergency basis, to take emergency action now to save the United States from being sucked into what is, in fact, a total collapse of the international Wall Street system; not just here in the United States, but in the entire northern trans-Atlantic region. And this sort of collapse would be the greatest collapse in history; and for that reason, he said, "Nothing else is of the priority of urgency, as the urgency of this Glass-Steagall bill."

So, I'm not going to say more, but what I'd like to do is ask Paul to come to the podium. I know he'll elaborate a little bit more on what Mr. LaRouche had to say earlier today, especially from the standpoint of what exactly is this bankruptcy of the Wall Street system. So, Paul.

Paul Gallagher: OK, thank you, Matt. So, this is indeed something really quite important, and full of the potential of change. If you think: What gross inequality of income, what shrinkage of wages, what shrinkage of the U.S. workforce, what loss of home ownership and household wealth in the United States, can't be traced to that period 20 years ago to 10 years ago when the major banks on Wall Street suddenly—with the regulations off, with Glass-Steagall gone—suddenly multiplied their size, relative to our economy, by five times in a matter of less than ten years? And at the same time, became impossibly complex and impossible to regulate for that reason.

When before in American history did you have an Attorney General who stated publicly, on two occasions, that he couldn't possibly prosecute one of these monsters, because if he were successful and found any of their executives or the bank itself guilty of crimes which might threaten its banking license, he would bring down the entire financial system and potentially bring down the U.S. economy? And so, he was going to leave them alone, despite the constantly multiplying evidence of crimes and riggings and fixings of every conceivable kind of market.

So, this really is extraordinarily important.

As you indicated, Lyndon LaRouche said today he sees nothing that has the urgency and the priority, at this moment, of this legislation; and that in his view, the members of the Senate who have taken this initiative to introduce the legislation should be recognized, they should be congratulated as heroes; and the passage of it—quickly—can avert an economic collapse in the United States, and enable the United States also to save Europe from economic collapse—I'll get into that.

LaRouche also noted today, that the action of those

LPAC-TV

Rep. Marcy Kaptur (D-Ohio) addresses the Congressional Progressive Caucus on her Glass-Steagall bill in 2011. The version of her bill in the current Congress (HR 381) has 60 cosponsors.

four sponsors took in the Senate repeats an action which the same four initially took in the previous session of Congress, roughly two years ago; but then very much *pro forma*; this time, in an entirely different way. With great urgency, suddenly, as an emergency action, ordered and coordinated with the Glass-Steagall legislation H.R.381 in the House, and with the sponsors of that legislation; and injected directly into the campaign to create a new Presidency in the United States.

So, it is no exaggeration to say that the rapid advance of the bill can open a new era for this country and for mankind. They took this action now with markets of every kind trembling and quaking; fully aware that a collapse of the entire U.S. economy is about to occur if these Glass-Steagall measures are not taken.

For example, Senator Warren, from her presentation on the floor: "The biggest banks continue to threaten our economy. The biggest banks are collectively much larger than they were before the crisis of 2007, and they continue to engage in dangerous practices that could once again crash our economy."

Then the response of candidate O'Malley, with the white paper, with the letter to Wall Street, with the immediate endorsement of the four Senators' action. Then the response of the head of the American labor move-

ment, Richard Trumka, urging that this be passed immediately, and saying that it would be a test the labor movement would put on candidates for their attitude toward this legislation. Other candidates will be responding, some of them, I think, quickly, because the consequences of not passing Glass-Steagall now would be fatal for the United States and really for the world. They know, these Senators, that the entire Wall Street system is in the process of a collapse; the European system as well is even further over the edge. And let's see why.

The Effect of Glass-Steagall

The Glass-Steagall Act's regulations basically had four components or four actions. First, the requirement that commercial banks, investment banks and broker-dealers, and thirdly insurance companies—which could underwrite insurance as well as sell it—had to be entirely separate from one another and could not share directors, ownership, or management. And any commercial bank or holding company which had interconnections with investment banks, broker-dealers, insurance companies, had to separate completely from them within a reasonable period.

Second, the definition of a significant range of securities and also financial derivatives bets as "not sufficiently closely incident to banking as to be proper to it"; and therefore, not to be permitted to commercial banks. The emphasis is: A significant range of securities and derivatives—the entire range of derivatives—are not permitted to commercial banks.

Third, the provision of Federal Deposit Insurance exclusively to support commercial banks and their depositors.

And fourth, the prohibition of transferring risky securities and derivatives within a holding company, onto the books of a federally-insured commercial bank; thereby causing these risky securities to become the responsibility, ultimately, of taxpayer funds. (**Figure 1**)

More than 60 years after it was passed, the Glass-Steagall organization of the commercial banking system ensured that no U.S. bank failure triggered failures or bail-outs of other banks. And after it was progressively eliminated in the course of the mid-'90s to '99, the effects in U.S. banking were absolutely dramatic. In 1999, the failure merely of a large hedge fund—not even large by today's standards, but large then—Long-Term Capital Management hedge fund, nearly broke the entire banking system then, because 55 banks had poured leveraged loans into its derivatives

FIGURE 1

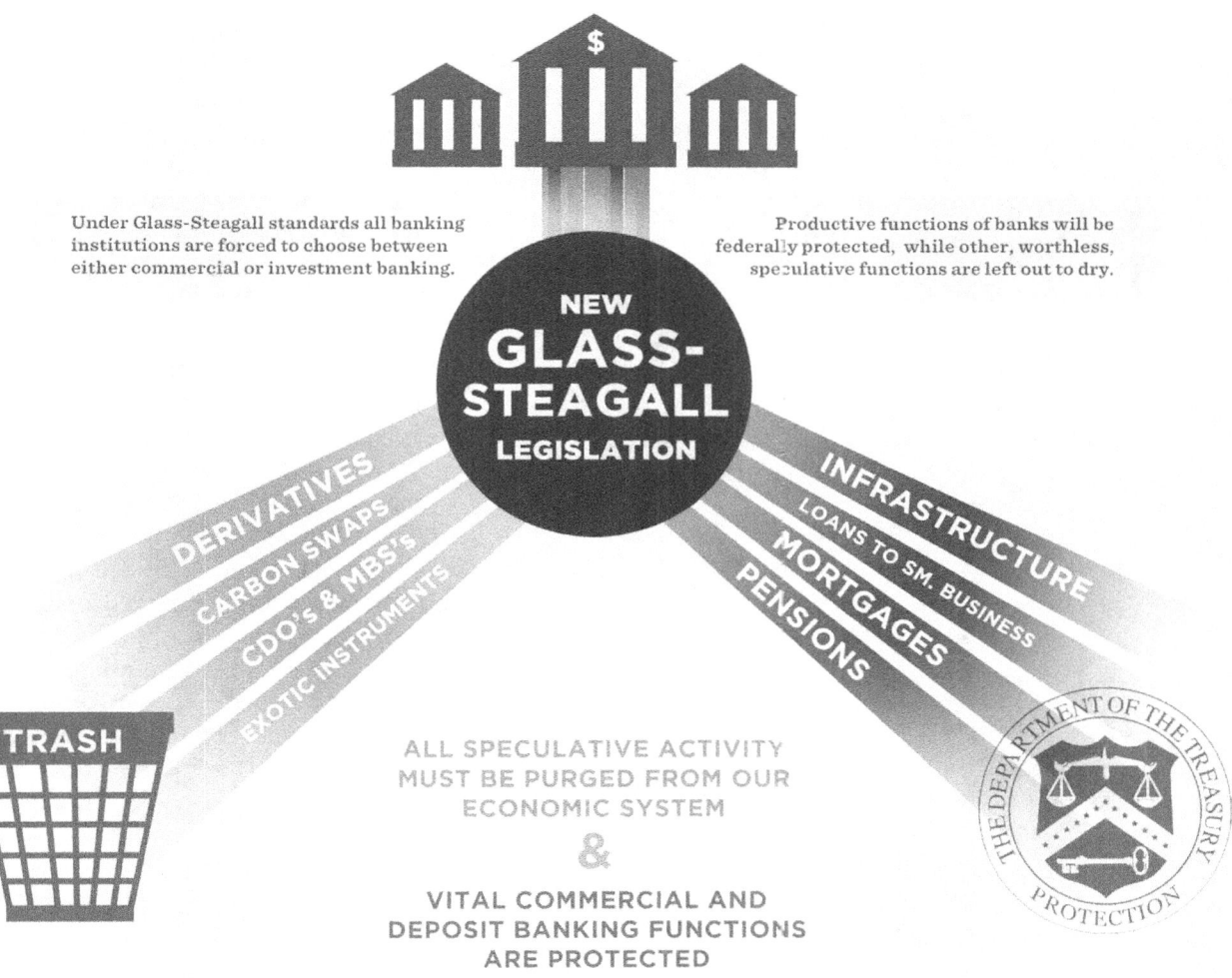

GLASS-STEAGALL
SEPARATE LEGITIMATE COMMERCIAL BANKING
from SPECULATIVE INVESTMENT FUNCTIONS

Under Glass-Steagall standards all banking institutions are forced to choose between either commercial or investment banking.

Productive functions of banks will be federally protected, while other, worthless, speculative functions are left out to dry.

NEW GLASS-STEAGALL LEGISLATION

DERIVATIVES
CARBON SWAPS
CDO's & MBS's
EXOTIC INSTRUMENTS

INFRASTRUCTURE
LOANS TO SM. BUSINESS
MORTGAGES
PENSIONS

TRASH

ALL SPECULATIVE ACTIVITY MUST BE PURGED FROM OUR ECONOMIC SYSTEM

&

VITAL COMMERCIAL AND DEPOSIT BANKING FUNCTIONS ARE PROTECTED

THE DEPARTMENT OF THE TREASURY · PROTECTION

bets; something which Glass-Steagall had prohibited them from doing.

The largest banks became impossibly complex—going from typically 100-200 subsidiaries to now typically 2,500 to 4,000 subsidiaries—buying and creating, overwhelmingly, security and broker-dealer vehicles. The derivatives markets exploded geometrically with the flow from these depository giants backing up derivative bets. It went from $57 trillion in notional value of the bets in 1997, to $700 trillion ten years later, according to the Bank for International Settlements.

And the largest banks became entirely interconnected with one another, particularly through making the same derivative bets, and therefore having the same

FIGURE 2
Derivatives

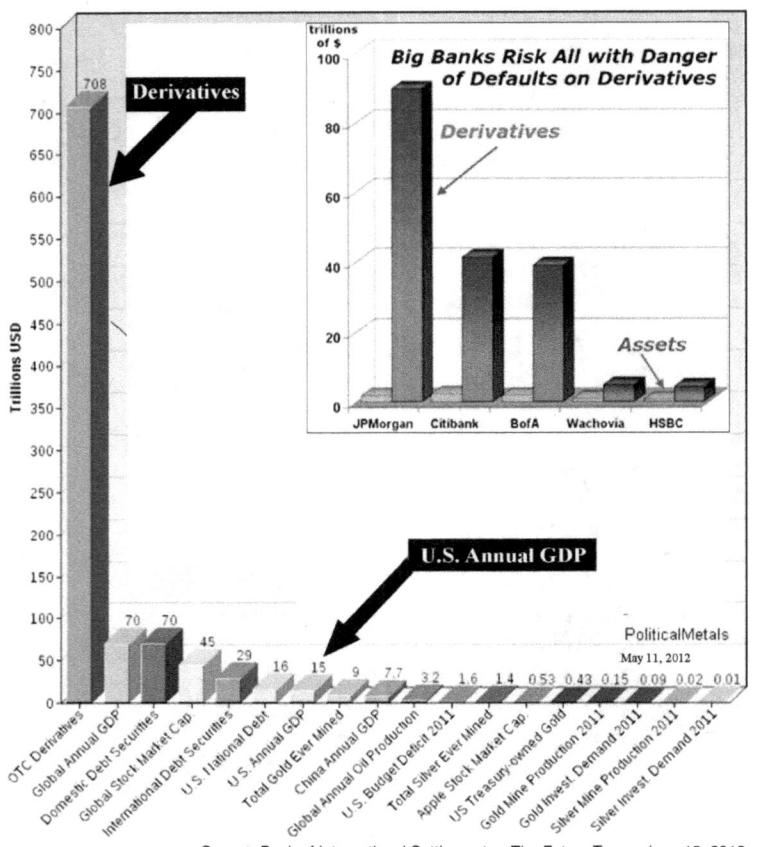

Source: Bank of International Settlements—The Future Tense, June 15, 2012.

If it was this bad in June 2012, you know it's much, much worse today.

derivatives exposures; while their leverage ratios—their assets to capital—was allowed to rise from 16:1 as a typical ratio to 30-35:1. And their loans fell to about half of their total assets; they stopped lending to the businesses and households while they got so much rapidly larger. Then they crashed and burned in 2008 and were saved by government agency credit to the financial system, which at one point reached $14 trillion, according the chairman of the Federal Deposit Insurance Corporation at that time.

Then, after being saved, the largest banks' lending plunged, their derivatives exposures became 30% larger than they were in 2007, and their total lending last year was below the level of six years earlier (**Figure 2**).

In the European Union, these figures are all much worse.

The situation a year ago, as described by a leading U.S. regulator, an official of the FDIC, on May 6, 2014, was "Compared to 2008, the largest financial firms today are larger, more complicated, more interconnected. The eight largest banking firms have assets that are the equivalent to 65% of the GDP of the United States. The average notional value of derivatives for the three largest banking firms at the end of 2013 exceeded $60 trillion *each*; a 30% increase over their level at the start of the crisis." He then went on to discuss their increased complexity, the way they use taxpayer insurance and what he calls "the federal safety net" to support their expansion across the globe and across the speculative securities markets and the derivatives markets. He said, "They remain excessively leveraged, with ratios on average of nearly 22:1."

So, that was a year ago. Recently, the same official warned that Wall Street's leveraged loans bubble had tripled to $800 billion, combined with a junk bond bubble that had reached $1.6 trillion; and that much of both of those were in the energy industry, which is being pushed into defaults and derivatives blow-outs by the collapse in the price of oil. And the $1.3 trillion auto loan market today, looks like the mortgage bubble in 2006; full of sub-prime, high-interest loans—extended long-term, because the buyers can't really afford to pay them.

And the condition of the largest banks in London and in the European Union is much worse. The trans-Atlantic banking system is heading for a general crash, despite, and because of, the endless money-printing and zero interest rate policy of the central bank.

For a Recovery, Bankrupt Wall Street

Now, here's how the Glass-Steagall legislation that we're talking about leads towards recovery. Based on the action that has been initiated in the Senate now, Congress—together with competent regulators—can do exactly what Franklin Roosevelt did in the beginning of his Presidency in March 1933, as Matthew referred.

The overall financial system at that time was in bankruptcy. Before doing anything else as President—and actually using a plan that had been developed by a Treasury Under-Secretary who was a Republican—he ordered a thorough investigation and auditing of every one of the 14,000 banks in the United States. That was done in a 10-day period; and by going through their books in that completely national dragnet way, they separated—and enabled the Treasury and Roosevelt himself to judge the separation—between the trash, toxic assets which made many of these banks bankrupt, and the sound commercial banks which had real productive assets.

This then opened the way for the recovery from the Great Depression; it was actually codified a few months later when Congress first passed Glass-Steagall in June of 1933. Roosevelt signed it, and at that point, this kind of examination of the soundness of the commercial lending of the commercial banks was going on every six months, which had gone on in that critical 10-day bank holiday under Roosevelt; which had enabled the banks to re-open and the recovery from the Depression collapse to begin.

And this is what Glass-Steagall, driving forward in both Houses of Congress, means today. You look at the derivatives provision alone, in what the Senators have just introduced: It will mean that, as the FDIC official identified for you, the roughly $225 trillion worth of derivatives bets, which are on the books of the six biggest U.S. bank holding companies, will have to go *off* those books, if there is any connection to insured commercial deposits, to bank deposits of ordinary depositors. That is clearly spelled out in the legislation.

Remember, they have 2,500-4,000 units each, under these bank holding companies. The great majority of those units are going to disappear, very quickly. Without the underpinning of the vast amounts of deposit money which is in these banks, and without Federal insurance backing these derivatives up, these things are going to be exposed for the bankrupts that they are. They're going to disappear.

Remember, just last December, when Wall Street and Obama rode roughshod over the Congress, in order to, in a desperation move, *keep* precisely the most risky and dangerous of all the derivatives that they had, including the commodity derivatives, keep them inside their commercial banking units, where the Federal insurance would be exposed to exactly those derivatives which were dying under the collapse of the oil price. And they forced Congress, by bribery, by direct phone calls, by, of course, the pressure of the President who backed this, they forced Congress to keep that protection—which the Glass-Steagall legislation is going to completely take away.

You're going to take all of this—no insured commercial bank will be able to underwrite these deriva-

Bush's Treasury Secretary Hank Paulson, browbeating Congress into passing the bank bailout in November 2008.

tives, under Glass-Steagall. No insured commercial bank will be able to play the securities markets. When this is enforced, we're going to find that the Wall Street casino is as bankrupt as it was in 1931-32. And, just as FDR's national inspection found that one-third of all the banks in the country were bankrupt, and closed down, the bankruptcy of much of what today's megabanks are holding under their holding companies, will be exposed.

So, with the dead debt flushed out, before it really begins to stink, the insured commercial banks under Glass-Steagall can potentially then invest, to contribute to a recovery of growth and productive employment.

This will be the greatest recovery action in the recent history of the United States. Congress has to use its authority to take an emergency action, now—not in the indefinite future, but now—and save the United States from being sucked into a total collapse of the international London/Wall Street financial system. We're witnessing a terminal bankruptcy.

A Change of Values

And, therefore, as LaRouche said, *nothing* is as urgent now, as this legislation. This is the future speaking to us, and the future is now being recognized by a significant group in the U.S. Senate. And the only way to give the U.S. economy a future, is by going back to Glass-Steagall, immediately, to open the door to investment in that future.

So, with Glass-Steagall, we can change the whole ordering of the relative values in the economies of the trans-Atlantic region. Don't worry about stock values, as people spend most of their time obsessing about now. Don't worry about Wall Street's interests. The entire Wall Street system is a fatal liability within the U.S. economic system; it is not an asset. It must simply be canceled. You can't have an institution which is that bankrupt, poisoning our system from within, aided and supported by Federal Reserve policy.

Look at the current investments in the United States, where the large businesses use *all* of the money that they borrow, and *all* of the profits that they earn, in order to buy their own stocks and stocks of other companies, in mergers, on the Wall Street markets. These large companies have become virtual appendages of the speculation by their big lenders, their big banks; while the small companies can't get any credit at all. And the result is, no capital investment, no productivity growth, therefore, no wage growth.

These bankrupt values have to be canceled. At that point, the United States will be liberated, and all these fictitious values can give us, as we throw them away, a fresh view of reality. And those activities which are real and productive, will suddenly rise in their relative value, as opposed to what has been dragging us down.

We will, for example, focus on the urgent necessity to invest in relieving the intensifying Western drought, by advanced technologies to produce and move water, including scientific frontiers involved in increasing total precipitation off the oceans onto the land masses of the Earth. We'll think of making travel rapid and comfortable, and freight travel rapid and cheap, by the kind of high-speed rail corridors across this continent, which have been built rapidly in Asia in the last decade and a half.

And the people of the United States, who have been suffering under this fraudulent system, will be given the opportunity to be productive again, and the opportunity to create the future.

So, we can lose no time in getting this done. This, again, takes priority in what has to be done in order to save the United States, and enable the United States to save Europe.

The 'Greek Debt' Drama

Ogden: And that's precisely what I want to pick up on, right here. Mr. LaRouche was saying earlier today, Wall Street is dead, but there's no reason why we need to have a funeral. We don't need to mourn the death of Wall Street. He said, this should be cause for jubilation, for celebration. And, he recommended, maybe, a traditional Irish wake. I think that might be more appropriate.

But, let me pick up on exactly what you just ended with.... You purge the system of these fictitious values. The entire system has been dying, suffocating, under the influence of these parasites that have been dragging it down, and distorting the entire relative idea of value within not only the United States economy, but within the entire trans-Atlantic economy as a system.

What Mr. LaRouche was emphatic about, is that this is not just Wall Street. This is representative of this entire trans-Atlantic financial system, which includes Europe as well. And, obviously, over the past week, the eyes of the world have been fixed upon Europe and the events that continue to unfold around Greece, there.

So, let me just present our institutional question for this week, which is on this subject, and ask Paul to respond. It reads as follows:

"Mr. LaRouche, your role in promoting a global Glass-Steagall, is widely recognized and appreciated. Now that it has been introduced into the United States Senate, how can Glass-Steagall help solve the European crisis, now coming to a showdown point with Greece?"

Gallagher: Well, Matt, I appreciate your reference to the Irish affair. 'Tis meself that will be after celebratin' it.

But on this question that's been given to us, it's simple and fundamental. First of all, there's not a Greek debt crisis. There's a London debt crisis. To give you an example, the big banks, which are all London centered—and people need to keep this in focus: Of all the derivatives bets in the world, the whole $700 billion, or $1 quadrillion in derivatives bets that there are in the world, half of all of them are in the London banks; and the $230 trillion notional value that our big banks have, is *half* of what's in the few monsters in London.

So, this is a London crisis, a London debt and derivatives crisis, and these banks, these mega-banks in Europe, have on their books $2 trillion in real estate-based bad loans, alone; not to mention the $500 billion European TARP program, basically, which loaned—EU500 billion, $550 billion—in bail-out funds to bail out these banks, but it wound up as the debt of Greece, and Portugal, and Ireland, and Spain, and some of the Eastern European countries.

So, they're into multiple, multiple trillions of bad

CC/Giannis Angelakis

One of millions of Greeks left homeless by EU austerity. This photo was taken on January 16, 2013.

debt on their books, and the debt of Greece, and its inability to pay this debt which bailed out these banks, which is triggering this crisis in recent weeks, is a very small part of it.

So anything could cause these banks to crash. They literally are dead monsters; they're lying in the road, in the way of any possible recovery from what's now effectively 10-year recession/depression collapse in Europe, a complete stagnation of all the economies there. And including a 10-year suppression of the industrial potential of Germany, which under the Merkel government is committing economic suicide, by keeping the clamps on the leading economy of Europe, as a result of all this unpayable debt which needs to be written down, and which these banks refuse to allow to be written down a single euro of it.

And within that, is lodged the Greek crisis, because the Greek government is one of the first, and with the biggest mass of debt, to arrive at the point when it's clearly unpayable—it's not going to be paid in anybody's lifetime.

Relief from Unpayable Debt

There've been many proposals for a replication on behalf of Greece, of the 1953 debt conference in London

which forgave more than half, at that time, of all the debt of Germany. And of course, the ironies are very pungent here, because it's Germany which is refusing, or taking the lead, the Merkel-Schäuble government is taking the lead in refusing debt relief to Greece, when Greece was one of the creditors which gave debt relief to Germany on a *far* larger scale, 60 years ago. And that debt relief— clearly everyone understands this— led immediately to the German economic miracle of the 1950s, and 1960s, and early 1970s.

So, it appears to be a complete perversity on the part of Merkel, Schäuble; it gives her the name of "Murky Merkel," because it appears that there's no possible reason—but there is a reason. My colleague Dean Andromidas and I wrote [an article] back in late January on the subject of this 1953 London Debt Conference, and why and how it could be applied to the problem not only of Greece, but of the half-dozen super-indebted countries in Europe see *EIR*, Jan. 23, 2015.

And we made clear, then, that the problem is the lack of Glass-Steagall: That is, in 1953, the banks of Europe were under Glass-Steagall principles. Most of the countries, after World War II, had actually passed copy-cat Glass-Steagall acts, laws, based on the U.S. law, and they had separation of their commercial banks from all of this casino speculation.

That put those banks in a position to allow debt to be written down, without setting off a bank panic and a chain-reaction collapse.

In addition, those banks were not in the derivatives markets to the extent of hundreds and hundreds of trillions of dollars of debts. So, a debt write-down on a large scale—60% of Germany's total debt going all the way back to the First World War period—could be agreed on, and could be implemented.

In Europe, that *cannot* happen until Glass-Steagall is done first. When the banks are put in that position where they can stand it, then that kind of debt write-down can take place.

What's happening now, what's being proposed, even by the Greek government now, after getting the support in this national referendum, is merely to add another roughly $60 billion, and with bank recapitalization probably $75 billion of debt on top of this European TARP that exists, of which almost none of the lending to those super-indebted countries by this European TARP has been paid back.

So you'd pile another $60-75 billion worth of debt onto that, and you'd say Greece owes this back in three years; with additional austerity—that's the proposal—with additional austerity measures applied in the meantime, which have already made it impossible for Greece to pay any debt, even on the scale of 30, 40, 50 years. So it's guaranteed that Greece will not be repaying any debts in three years; so this is a proposal to increase the unpayable debt burden in the London-centered banking system, by another $60 billion to $75 billion. It is completely unworkable.

But, it's ironic and very useful, that the more Angela Merkel insists—"No debt write-down for Greece, not a euro"—the more she insists, the more articles appear, reminding her, in the German press as well, reminding her that 60 years ago Germany got not just debt relief, but 60% of its debt wiped away completely, and then went on to an economic miracle which made it the leading economic power in Europe ever since; and put it in a position to do extraordinary things with regard to Eurasian development as a whole.

So that irony is very useful. And if it contributes to Merkel's departure from office quickly, it would be even more useful.

But again, it is not soluble, except Glass-Steagall coming from the United States—and here's, again, as LaRouche said immediately about this Senate introduction of the already-existing House bill—that it's not just opening up the United States for an economic recovery. It's life-or-death for Europe now. If Europe collapses completely, the world is in trouble. Glass-Steagall's enactment now, puts the United States in a position to force that through all over Europe, and actually knock out this debt problem that is completely strangling and collapsing the European economies, and let them grow as well.

So, it means, really—this collapse in Europe—that it's the British banking empire that's going down, and there's room for a renewal, there's room for a fresh start on economic productivity and growth, and the United States can open that up for Europe by the Glass-Steagall Act which was just introduced in the Senate in the U.S.

A Role in the BRICS' New Order

Ogden: Now, as I said earlier, what Mr. LaRouche stated to us, was the restoration of Glass-Steagall and the cancellation of this entire fraudulent gambling system that's based in Wall Street, portends a new era for mankind. And I think this question of how does the restoration of Glass-Steagall open up for us this new era of productivity, this new era of a science-driver for the planet as a whole, is one that I want to address before we conclude tonight's discussion.

And I especially want to go back to what Paul brought up earlier, when Mr. LaRouche was describing this total reordering of relative values in the trans-Atlantic system; what he described as a cancellation of this fictitious value and a restoration of sanity, to what we define as "value," what we deem economically valuable. And when you look at this type of total reordering of values, that would be precipitated by a Glass-Steagall cancellation of this fraudulent system on Wall Street, how that would be applied not only in the United States, but also, in Europe, and how that would play in the entire world.

Mr. LaRouche said: Look at the role of China and Russia, especially. These nations as we speak, already, are unleashing productive forces that are unprecedented in world history. They're unprecedented in their scope, of both accomplishment already, but also, what they aim to accomplish, in the future. Look at the Chinese lunar program as an example, with the helium-3 component. These are absolutely crucial. And this has the power to initiate a science-driver era for the planet, and again, would create an explosion of productivity that has never before been seen.

You could also, as Paul just mentioned, look at the potential relationship between Germany and Russia, if Merkel and Schäuble and those like them can be defeated. We can reorder the economies of Europe, as a whole.

And so, if you look at the actions by the BRICS countries, for example, that they've taken during their recent summit this week: Simultaneous with all of these other developments occurring, the BRICS were meeting for their Seventh Summit in Ufa, Russia this week. This portends a great future, a new international order for mankind. And Glass-Steagall has a crucial role to play in that, here in the United States.

So as I said, simultaneous with the introduction of Glass-Steagall into the Senate, simultaneous with what we were just discussing about the events in Europe, the

kremlin.ru

Russian President Vladimir Putin at the 7th BRICS Summit in Ufa, Russia on July 9.

leaders of the BRICS nations—Brazil, Russia, India, China, and South Africa—*together* with the leaders, and I think, the observers, of the SCO (the Shanghai Cooperation Organization), both of these organizations were meeting together in Ufa, Russia.... This occurred almost exactly a year after the Fortaleza summit last year in Brazil, which happened in mid-July.

The New Development Bank, which was agreed to at the Fortaleza Summit last year, is now officially up and running. And you have the integration between the BRICS, the SCO, also the Chinese New Silk Road initiative, and the Russian Eurasian Economic Union [EAEU] initiative: All of these are now being integrated, and this integration is being solidified and is being recognized as being indicative, of a total realignment of the planet, and a creation of a new, international economic *and* strategic order.

So, for example, there was a headline today in *The Hindu*, which is one of the leading newspapers out of India, which read as follows: "BRICS, SCO, EAEU Can Define New World Order: China, Russia." And I just want to read a few sentences from the beginning of this article, because I think it aptly describes exactly what just occurred, in Ufa this week. The article starts by saying:

"China and Russia have described BRICS, the Shanghai Cooperation Organization (SCO) and the Eurasian Economic Union (EAEU) as the core of a new

international order, defined by a multipolar world.

"Far from being rival organizations, the three groupings should be looking at their ties from a 'strategic and long-term perspective,' Xinhua reported that Chinese President Xi Jinping said." Xi Jinping "briefed leaders of the three organizations on China's One Belt, One Road" initiative (which is the Silk Road initiative), "the establishment of the Asian Infrastructure Investment Bank (AIIB) and the $40 billion Silk Road Fund," and "Mr. Xi underscored the convergence in the development strategies of the three groupings."

The article continues later to say:

Echoing Mr. Xi's perceptions, Russian President Vladimir Putin, also said at Ufa ... that the three groupings can premise an 'a powerful economic breakthrough."

"There is no doubt," Mr. Putin said, "we have all necessary premises to expand the horizons of mutually beneficial cooperation, to join together our raw material resources, human capital and huge consumer markets for a powerful economic spurt."

Russia's TASS news agency also quoted Mr. Putin as saying that the Eurasian continent had vast transit potential. He pointed to 'the construction of new efficient transport and logistics chains, in particular, the implementation of the initiative of the Silk Road Economic Belt and the development of transportation in the eastern part of Russia and Siberia. This may link the rapidly growing markets in Asia and Europe's economies, mature, rich in industrial and technological achievements. At the same time, this will allow our countries to become more commercially viable in ... creating new jobs, for advanced enterprises."

So that's just a taste of what is coming out of this BRICS summit that occurred this past week in Russia. And clearly, the United States must join this new, "win-win" economic order, as it's been called by Xi Jinping.

Which we will be free to do, once we've eliminated the Wall Street parasitical system, by restoring Glass-Steagall. Obviously, this is the subject of a petition which has been circulating for several months now and continues to be circulated by the Schiller Institute, which is called "The U.S. and Europe Must Have the Courage to Reject Geopolitics and Collaborate with the BRICS," which was featured in a *very* significant way on the eve of this BRICS summit, July 6, by the Russian news outlet Sputnik, which conducted an interview with Helga Zepp-LaRouche, which it published in printed form and also ran as a full 15-minute segment live on Sputnik Radio; Helga Zepp-LaRouche, the chairwoman of the Schiller Institute and the initiator of the petition. And this is available on the LaRouche PAC site also.

Building Infrastructure

Now, what I just want to ask Paul to conclude with, and address briefly in the context of what I just laid out, is the point that Mr. LaRouche made in his remarks earlier: After Glass-Steagall, what's next? How do we replicate what Franklin Roosevelt did in his first term as President? What do we learn from the lessons that Alexander Hamilton, our first Treasury Secretary, taught us, the "hero of New York," as Mr. LaRouche identified him today? And how does the United States join the BRICS?

Gallagher: Well, that really was a crucial part of our discussion of this issue today, with Lyndon LaRouche, because obviously, the opening of this legislation's introduction in the Senate, and the possibility of its rapidly passing on an emergency basis in this crash, opens up, then, what the rest of the world, or at least a significant part of the world that you're talking about, is already engaged in; it opens it up for the United States and for Europe, the trans-Atlantic sector as a whole, you might call it, which are flat on their economic rearends.

These institutions, new international development banks which are being set up by India, Russia, China, the BRICS nations, and others—57 countries joined what was originally the Asian Infrastructure Investment Bank (AIIB), is now a bank backed by 57 countries, against the opposition of the Obama administra-

tion—; so this is being done. And the avowed purpose of these new international development banks is financing modern infrastructure, high-speed rail, modern power infrastructure, water management, water production, making "connectivity" as they call it now; and no country in the world needs this worse than the United States!

We have a drought which is threatening to cut off one-third of the United States from the rest of the country—the most productive part of it—and depopulate it and leave it as essentially a desertifying and eventually a desert area. This is a threat to the national economy of a sort which very few nations face. And we are doing *nothing* about it! President Obama doesn't even discuss the issue! We have the crazy governor of California, who proposes exactly that kind of depopulation, and in the process, poor people dying from lack of water and disease in the Central Valley of California and elsewhere; and we do nothing about it.

And everyone knows that we do nothing, year after year after year, about the breakthrough areas of high-technology economic infrastructure, which *alone* can really raise productivity in the economy again, and thereby reestablish productive employment, and remunerative employment, because it is on a rising level of productivity: This has to be done.

Enter Alexander Hamilton

We're discussing here, tonight, with all of you, as if you were members of Congress, the principles and the methods by which Glass-Steagall worked in the past, and will work now to open this possibility of investment in economic recovery, to clean away the trash, of many, many trillions of dollars of unpayable debt.

But, there's an even bigger prospect in front of us in the future: You have to consider that 200 and some years ago, the Congress of the United States was capable of debating, deliberating and passing, two pieces of legislation introduced to it by Alexander Hamilton: The Act for the Establishment of Public Credit; and the Act for the Creation of a National Bank. And yet, today, there's not a single member of Congress who understands anything about Alexander Hamilton's economics!

So there is *really* quite a future development ahead of us, here, because then was a time when we actually had elected officials, who were able to understand national credit. They may not all have all understood it equally, they debated it, but they were able to under-

A sketch of Alexander Hamilton's Bank of the United States, as it was erected in Philadelphia in 1797.

stand, act, pass it through: Get national credit created and of course, the genius of all of that, as Lyn said, the "hero of New York," was Alexander Hamilton, who absolutely has to remain on the $10 bill. And as one columnist said, "He should be on all the currency, because he invented it." Not just on the $10 bill.

What is involved in this, really, starts with his urgent reorganization of what was then unpayable debt of the United States and its constituent states, which had accumulated these debts as colonies when they were fighting for their independence, and then had accumulated more unpayable debts, in the Confederation period as states, because of the lack of an effective federal government.

Hamilton was able to devise the principles by which a debt reorganization, of debt that couldn't be paid at the time it was due; a debt reorganization could actually be used to create a National Bank which could inject credit into an economy, into productive activity—particularly at that time, roads, canals, the most important infrastructure of that time. And provided that this debt was given a means of its "extinguishment" as he said, a means, over a longer period of time, to reliably pay it off, then that debt would be a national blessing, and would actually be usable as credit through a National Bank which would be large enough, but yet, limited in what it did to productive lending, so that it could actually drive the science drivers and the technology drivers

for the economy as a whole.

That was part of Hamilton's genius. But he also understood something which requires transformation on an even deeper level in the United States, now. He understood that we, at that time, despite the high level of education of the colonists and of the citizens of the United States in 1790—much higher than comparable citizens in England, for example—despite that, they were not very productive in their economic activity because the country essentially had no division of labor; it was essentially a nation of husbandry, a nation of farmers, who were in the process of expanding to the West and farming, and farming, and farming.

And Hamilton began, for the first time in U.S. debate, to introduce the ideas that a higher division of labor, a greater progress of scientific inventions into technology and into labor, and a greater ability of exchange between various divisions of manufacturing, labor, and agriculture, that this could provide scientific and technological progress in *both* branches—agriculture and manufacturing—and that it, as he said, provided the most fertile ground for the spiritual and intellectual development of the most inventive souls in the population; provided that there were banks there. Provided that there were banks there, and credit was generated, and these kinds of inventions could be realized.

And Hamilton, in that process, defined and created for the first time, what we call today a "commercial bank"; it's really an invention of Alexander Hamilton. Before that, banks were either merchant banks, which means they financed the largest international companies in their trading and in their colonization; or, they were banks that speculated in government debt.

There was no such thing as what Hamilton created, which was, first with the Bank of North America, and then the First National Bank, and then with a number of other banks; and by the time he wrote the *Report on Manufactures* in 1792, he was pointing to the fact that banks were multiplying, and that the purpose of these banks was to lend to the husbandman, the farmer, to the manufacturer, and to the households of both.

And his National Bank, which he had created from this debt reorganization, was itself not lending to or speculating in government debt; it was a national bank not created to buy the government's debt, and in fact it was not allowed to, by its charter. And that was true of the Second Bank, which was based on Hamilton's principles again, and would have been true of the Third Bank when Henry Clay designed it in 1841; it was true of Lincoln's greenback policy: This has been the basis of creation of credit by every real Presidential President that we have had, from Washington, to Quincy Adams, to Lincoln, to FDR and JFK, who understood this to a significant degree.

And these Hamiltonian methods of dealing with unpayable debt, including writing it off, in part; reorganizing it in part into an institution that can get backing and turn it into credit; these methods which Hamilton pioneered, resulted in the fact that the United States, throughout the Nineteenth Century—and really until the Depression—enjoyed thousands and thousands, and *tens* of thousands of banks, on a small scale, financing the advance of local industry, homeownership, agriculture, and the advance of science and technology in each of these branches; and that's exactly how Hamilton foresaw the development of the United States, nearly 250 years ago.

A Study for Congress

This is what is opened up by getting Glass-Steagall now through both Houses of Congress, bankrupting Wall Street, in order to get rid of this unpayable debt and its derivatives betting on top of it; above all, getting us out of the business of guaranteeing the derivatives bets of the banking casino. Then you get to Hamilton's methods of what the United States needs more critically than any other nation in the world, really, and that is, large-scale, high-technology transportation, connection, water, power, infrastructure, connecting us across the Bering Strait, into the Eurasian high-speed rail networks which have been built over the last 15 years; and really providing productive employment for our population.

We've got to go back to Hamilton. But the door is open for doing that, by the action that the Senators have taken, and the rapid progress of Glass-Steagall through both Houses now.

Ogden: And Mr. LaRouche underscored the four reports that were written by Hamilton: The *Report on Manufactures*, the *Report on Public Credit*, the *Report on a National Bank*, and the *Argument for the Constitutionality of a National Bank*, which are not classified, not redacted, they're in the public domain; they're available for anybody to read, and they're even written in English.

Gallagher: You can get them all in one book.

Ogden: Even a member of Congress can study these.

So I think in conclusion, we can celebrate the introduction of Glass-Steagall in the Senate; we can mobilize like Hell to pass this as soon as possible. We can celebrate the death of bankrupt Wall Street system, and we can always remember, that the name of the future, is Alexander Hamilton.

With that said, I'd like to thank all of you for joining us here today; I'd like to thank Paul for joining me here in the studio, and I would like to invite you to please stay tuned to larouchepac.com. If you are in the New York area, there's another like dialogue via video with Mr. LaRouche tomorrow afternoon, Saturday, in which you can participate by contacting our office up there.

Thank you all for joining us tonight, and please tune in next week.

LAROUCHE PAC SCIENTIFIC
RESEARCH TEAM REPORT

Towards a Galactic Science Driver

CONTENTS

I. What is A Galactic Science Driver?

by Benjamin Deniston

June 21, 2015

In the spring of 2015 the LaRouche PAC science team defined a perspective for addressing the water crisis in California and other locations based on recently developing insights into the role of our Galactic System in shaping climate, weather, and the behavior of the water cycle on Earth.[1] However, this is just one aspect of understanding our Galactic System, and how it relates to processes in our Solar System and on Earth. In this report we will recognize that galactic water perspective as just one expression of a deeper relation to our Galactic System. In what follows we will examine a broader perspective for understanding the higher-order system which is our Galaxy, in pursuit of a universal physical principle of the Galactic System.

Over the recent months Lyndon LaRouche has increasingly emphasized the need for a science driver program focused on understanding the Galaxy.

Here we will present various paths of investigation into scientific frontiers associated with the Galaxy, but before getting to that, we must emphasize a clarification on the meaning of a science driver program.

This is different than a technology driver, or an engineering driver, or a physical economic driver. That is not to say those are not important—they are needed elements of general human progress. However, none of them are designed to achieve the same thing as a science driver (although there can be inherent overlap).

The former drivers focus on increasing the useful applications of known scientific principles, to improve the ability to utilize known principles, and to expand the scale of national utilization of those potentials. A science driver focuses on pursuing new fundamental principles, principles existing outside the entire domain of operation of these other drivers.

This is the same distinction underlying many people's miSunderstanding of LaRouche's emphasis that "there has been no progress in science, no practiced progress in science since the beginning of the Twentieth Century."

Einstein and Planck changed our fundamental understanding of the Universe. The age of space travel, smart phones, satellites, and silicon has been built upon that new understanding of the Universe. While our ability to pursue certain tracks of engineering and technological development has greatly improved, there have been no new fundamental scientific revolutions—no new Einsteins, no new Leibnizs, no new Keplers. Even worse, the understanding of true science has not merely stagnated, it has collapsed.

As Jason Ross has been developing, the understanding of how it is that the human mind comes to create and develop true science has profoundly degenerated—with a cult belief in mathematics, logic, and formal systems increasingly overtaking any true insight into human creativity.[2] The Twentieth Century has seen a profound degeneration in the very understanding of our

---

1. "New Perspectives on the Western Water Crisis,", April 3, 2015; "Atmospheric Moisture Control," *EIR*, April 17, 2015.

2. "Man's True Nature," by Jason Ross, *EIR*, May 1, 2015.

own nature as mankind, as expressed most clearly in modern cultural and artistic expressions.[3]

This is not merely unfortunate, it is existential. This is a rejection of the very essential capability which defines mankind as distinct from the animals—predefining a path into a new dark age.

So Why the Galaxy?

Start with Nicholas of Cusa's conception of the ordering of the Universe.[4] Truth (knowledge) is not developed through the accumulation of self-defined and self-contained facts—it is developed by a unique power of the human mind to create increasingly less-imperfect conceptions of the wholes which create the facts (sometimes even seemingly contradictory or inconsistent facts). This is developed by the unique human creative capability to create valid higher-order conceptions of the unsensed causes (rather than simply recording sensed effects). Scientific understanding of causality in the Universe does not come from a Newton-Laplace style accumulation of measurements of an increasing number of individual parts; it comes from the discovery of successive higher-order unifications which determine the lower-order multiplications.

Here we will work from a developing thesis, first published in the article, "Science For A New Paradigm: Time for a Solar Noösphere."[5] By that thesis, the present scientific knowledge level of mankind could be broadly classified as a "stellar system level." For example, the revolutionary understanding of the equivalence of matter and energy underlines the energetic activity of our star, the Sun; an adequate understanding of the physics of these processes requires the understanding of the quantization of activity in the very small; the relativistic understanding of gravitation underlies the orbital organization of the Solar System's bodies.

Nicholas of Cusa (1401–1464), founder of modern science and leading organizer of the Renaissance, whom Vernadsky describes elsewhere as "one of the most original and prodigious minds of his time."

But, what subsumes the Solar System? From what was the Solar System created, and what is the physics associated with that higher-order process?

Consistent with the destructive intervention by David Hilbert and Bertrand Russell (to call for the axiomatization of mathematical and scientific thought), the current narrative taught in schools is that everything from the Galaxy to the entire Universe will be explained in the mechanisms and capabilities associated with this stellar-level science.

Here that assumption will be rejected—both on the basis of its dubious, unnatural origins, and on the basis of the evidence and anomalies provided by the studies of our Galaxy, pointing to the potentialities of new levels of science beyond our current stellar-level conception.

Leaving the treatment of the inherently dubious nature of this rejected assumption to other locations,[6] in this report we will review two categorical tracks of evidence which could converge upon a new galactic-level of science.

Since our Solar System is a subsumed component of the higher-order Galactic System one area of study is the history of the Earth and the Solar System, seeking indications of how they have responded to and been influenced by the higher-order Galactic System. The other track focuses on properties of the large-scale structure of the Galaxy itself.

The remainder of this introductory article will briefly review examples of possible studies in each category. This will be followed by additional articles addressing some of these studies in more depth.

Response of Stellar Systems to Changing Galactic Environments

Improving records of climatic, biospheric, and geophysical activity on Earth (and in some limited cases on other planetary bodies as well) provide long histories of variations and changes of these systems. In a number of

---

3. See the May 20, 2015 LaRouche PAC A New Paradigm for Mankind show, "Mankind Is Not An Animal."

4. *De Docta Ignorantia*, Nicholas of Cusa, 1440.

5. November 28, 2014 issue of Executive Intelligence Review.

6. See, "Man's True Nature," Jason Ross (*EIR*, May 1, 2015) and upcoming work by Ross.

cases the changes of these systems correspond quite well with what is presently known about the travels of our Solar System through our Galaxy, and with the associated changes in the galactic environment. In some cases there are hypotheses for the mechanisms by which a changing galactic environment can affect these planetary systems; in other cases the current scientific paradigm fails to provide adequate hypotheses.

Evidence for such responses can be seen in three types of systems (climate systems, biospheric systems, and geophysical systems), though they are not mutually exclusive, and clearly interact. In certain cases, perhaps some of the most provocative evidence could come from indications of separate planetary bodies responding and reacting simultaneously—indicating that each planetary body would be responding independently to the same external, cosmic influence.

Climate and Weather

The collaborative work of scientists Henrik Svensmark, Nir Shaviv, and their associates has provided a growing body of evidence showing that the different galactic environments experienced by the Earth have a profound effect on the Earth's climate system. First, it was shown that periods of major ice ages (spanning tens of millions of years) corresponded with the passages of the Solar System through our Galaxy's spiral arms.[7] More recently it has also been shown that the cyclical motion of our Solar System above and the galactic plane also corresponds with temperature variations (on a cycle of about 30 mil-

NASA

Artist's rendering of our Milky Way Galaxy, with the galactic coordinate system, Solar System location, and spiral arms labeled.

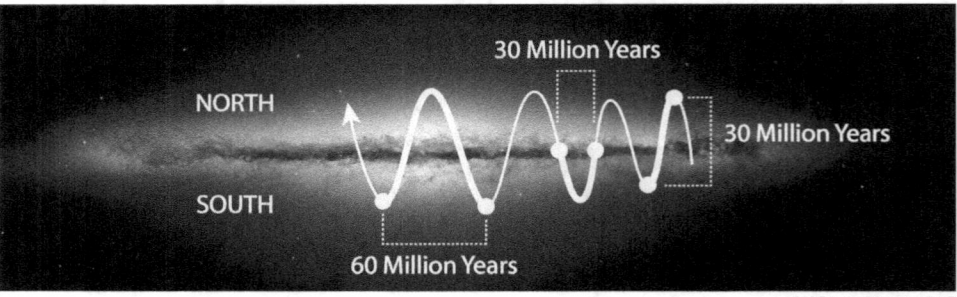

NASA, LaRouche PAC

Side view of a spiral galaxy, with an exaggerated illustration of the motion of the Solar System above and below the galactic disk.

lion years).[8] They have developed a solid theory that this galactically-induced climate change is mediated through variations in the galactic cosmic radiation environment of our Solar System, our Earth, and our Earth's thin atmosphere—controlling the behavior of

---

7. See "Celestial driver of Phanerozoic climate?" Nir Shaviv and Ján Veizer, GSA Today, July 2003.

8. "Is the Solar System's Galactic Motion Imprinted in the Phanerozoic Climate?" Nir J. Shaviv, Andreas Prokoph, & Jan Veizer, Nature Science Reports, August 21, 2014.

Stratocumulus Clouds Over Pacific, January 2013. Evidence now shows that high energy galactic cosmic rays play a significant role in cloud formation.

2005 David Monniaux

Tyrannosaurus rex at the Palais de la Découverte, Paris. Tyrannosaurus rex was just one of billions of animal species which have gone extinct.

atmospheric water vapor, cloud formation, and, thereby, the climate.

This overall framework provides the basis for an understanding of how mankind can manage these conditions himself—controlling aspects of the weather, rainfall, and climate.[9]

Additional insights could be provided by an examination of changes in the climate and weather systems of different planetary bodies, in an attempt to define indications of external factors influencing and controlling certain aspects of entire planetary systems (see "Solar System Weather Changes Challenge Conventional Theories," by Meghan Rouillard).

Evolution of Living Matter on Earth

A 2005 study showed very strong cycles of rise and fall in the number of distinct fossilized species over the past 540 million years—a stronger cycle of 62 million years and a weaker but still significant cycle of 140 million years.[10] Both of these cycles of rise and fall in bio-

diversity correspond (in period and phase) with these same two cyclical aspects of our Solar System's motion through the Galaxy (mentioned just above)—the motion above and below the galactic plane and the passage through the spiral arms. While this correspondence has been noted, the cause for such a relation is more ambiguous. Additional studies have also shown evidence for a relation between the galactic environment and the evolutionary development of living matter, proposing a few possible mechanisms. Svensmark has shown a relation between changing galactic environments (characterized by the expected changing rate of nearby supernovae) and the overall productivity of the biosphere—hypothesizing that the relation is mediated through climate change.[11] Another scientist has examined a possible periodicity in mass extinction events which might correspond with the periodic passage of our Solar System through the Galaxy's central disk—hypothesizing that this could perturb and provoke periodic comet impacts.[12]

Even with these proposed mechanisms, there is much ambiguity for how and why such a galactic relation to evolution would exist, perhaps reflecting a profound lack of understanding about the fundamental nature of living processes and/or of our Galactic System. The work of Vladimir Vernadsky provides an

9. See the LaRouche PAC show, A New Paradigm for Mankind, for May 6, 2015 and for May 13, 2015; also published in EIR, May 15, 2015 ("Galactic Man: Shadow versus Principle"), and May 22, 2015 ("Bringing the Rain").

10. "Cycles in fossil diversity," Rohde and Muller, March 10, 2005, Nature, Vol. 434.

11. "Evidence of nearby supernovae affecting life on Earth," Henrik Svensmark, Monthly Notices of the Royal Astronomical Society, Volume 423, Issue 2, pages 1234-1253, June 2012.

12. "Disc dark matter in the Galaxy and potential cycles of extraterrestrial impacts, mass extinctions and geological events," Michael R. Rampino, February 18, 2015, Monthly Notices of the Royal Astronomical Society, Vol. 448, Issue 2.

epistemologically better framework for approaching this question (see "A Vernadskian Reconsideration of Galactic Cycles and Evolution," republished as a contribution to this present report[13]).

Geophysical Activity

Studies have also shown a provocative correlation between records of periodic geophysical activity on Earth, the evolutionary development of living matter, and the motion of the Solar System above and below the galactic plane—all approximating the same ~60 million year periodicity.[14] Because the current stellar-level scientific paradigm lacks adequate hypotheses for how the influence of the Galactic System could affect the internal dynamics of planetary bodies, most authors touching upon this subject tend to put little (if any) emphasis on the galactic correlation to geophysical activity. However, at least one study has cited a theoretical mechanism by which the varying galactic environments experienced by the Earth could induce a type of geophysical activity (in this case volcanism).[15]

Returning to the method of comparing different planetary bodies for indications of correlated activity provides some preliminary but provocative indications that recent (in geological time) periods of large-scale volcanism on Earth correspond quite well with the most recent periods of volcanism on the moon—indicating a coordinated response of seemingly independent planetary bodies, pointing to external cosmic influences on timescales corresponding to galactic variations (see "Earth-Moon Comparative Planetology," in this report).

Taken together we see indications that the long-term changes and development of various processes on Earth (and perhaps on other planetary bodies)—from geophysical activity, to climate and

Wikicommons: Williamborg

Three Devil's grade in Moses Coulee, Washington is part of the Columbia River Large Igneous Province (LIP). Lips are produced when massive amounts of hot magma extrudes from inside the Earth and flows over the surface.

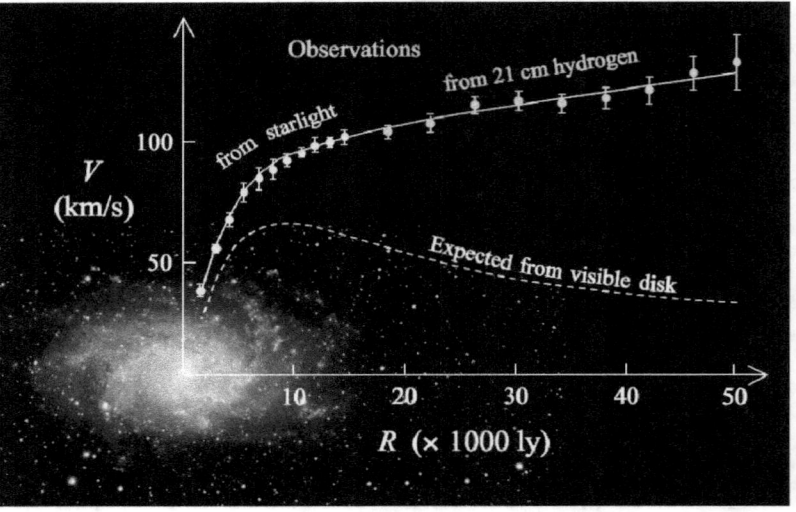
Wikimedia Commons:Stefania.deluca

The orbital speed measured at different distances compared with what would be expected for the galaxy M33.

weather, to the evolutionary development of living matter on Earth—correspond with the changing galactic environment experienced by the Solar System.

As stated above, in some of these cases there are hypotheses for how this interaction may occur; in other cases the current scientific paradigm fails to produce adequate hypotheses. The point is not to expect a resolution from within the existing framework, but to seek the clues indicating a higher level galactic principle, subsuming the present scientific level. The response of Earth systems (and potentially other planetary bodies) to changing galactic environments is only one path of

---

13. Originally published in *EIR*, May 22, 2015
14. "An ~60-Million-Year Periodicity Is Common to Marine 87Sr/86Sr, Fossil Biodiversity, and Large-Scale Sedimentation: What Does the Periodicity Reflect?" Melott, Bambach, et al, Journal of Geology, Vol. 120, No. 2 (March 2012),
15. "Disc dark matter in the Galaxy and potential cycles of extraterrestrial impacts, mass extinctions and geological events," Michael R. Rampino, February 18, 2015, Monthly Notices of the Royal Astronomical Society, Vol. 448, Issue 2.

pursuit of this galactic principle—we can also examine the large-scale, global dynamics and features of Galactic Systems as a whole.

Global Galactic Structure, Dynamics, and Singularities

Certain characteristics of galaxies, when studied as single systems, remain outside the scope of explanation within the current stellar-level science. Many characteristics could possibly be included, but here we will review just a few: evidence for an effect associated with the investigations into so-called dark matter; evidence for a large-scale coherence in the global organization of galactic systems; and the association of this coherence with a physical singularity (often referred to as a supermassive black hole).

These phenomena challenge our current conceptions of causality (expressed across space and time on these scales), and the energy flux density limits of reactions.

So-Called 'Dark Matter'

For decades it has been known that the orbital periods of stars in the outer regions of galaxies are much faster than can be explained by the amount of mass which can presently be detected in the respective galaxies. This has given rise to speculations and investigations into hypothetical types of matter which haven't been able to be detected, but which exert gravitational effects—so-called dark matter. Others view this as evidence that our understanding of gravity is not complete, and needs to be modified when expressed on galactic scales.

From the standpoint of the thesis of this report, we should start with the original discovery of universal gravitation, as done by Kepler in his discovery of the harmonic organization of the Solar System as a single system. To assert that we can take the mathematical interpretation of that discovery, and apply it to the organization of the higher order system of a galaxy, is an assumption—one which could very well be invalid. The so-called dark matter paradox might only be resolved with a discovery of a higher-order principle governing the harmonic organization for the Galactic System as a whole.

M-Sigma Relation

Another indication of a higher-order principle governing the structure of a single galactic system is referred to as the "M-sigma" relation (or the black hole-bulge relation). This is an indication that the mass of a supermassive object found at the center of most galaxies (thought to be a supermassive black hole) is always in a very direct proportion with the mass of the spherical bulge structure of the host galaxy. A larger galaxy, with a larger bulge, will have a larger supermassive central object, and a smaller galaxy, with a smaller bulge, will have a smaller supermassive central object.

At first this would intuitively seem to make sense. However, because the scales are so different, it is not understood how either the supermassive central object could exert control over the bulge, or how the bulge could exert control over the supermassive central object (or how they could both be subject to the same external control). Moreover, this is not a broad relation; it is a very tight proportion, holding across many orders of magnitude of size of different galaxies.

Within the existing mechanisms available to the current level of stellar science, it is not yet clear how to explain this relationship—nor is it clear that it could be explained within the current framework. Perhaps a new level of science is required (see "Singularities and Supermassive Black Holes," in this report).

A Physical Singularity?

This takes us to another particularly interesting area of investigation: the phenomena referred to as supermassive black holes. The very idea of a black hole is inherently an anomalous phenomenon.

According to the mathematical interpretation in general relativity, a black hole is a location where the equations explaining space and time go to infinity (a singularity), and attempts to understand the physics break down. This is an unambiguous boundary marking the limits of present knowledge—what happens here (and beyond here) is not only unknown; it is unknowable in the present stellar-level scientific framework, and will require a new revolution in science to discover (see "Singularities and Supermassive Black Holes," in this report).

Active Galactic Nuclei

What makes this even more interesting is the association of supermassive central objects (physical singularities) with a phenomenon known as active galactic nuclei.

In a small percentage of observable galaxies, the very central region of the core is incredibly active and

NASA

Galaxy NGC 4414.

only be explained by an as-yet-unknown organizing principle.

Most important will be unexpected convergence of multiple tracks which were thought to be independent.

The goal is to discover a new principle which subsumes current notions—by this very nature (with respect to current knowledge) its character, and how and why it subsumes what notions, is not deducible before its discovery.

We can be guided by certain general epistemological insights (following the principles of the foundations of modern science developed by Cusa), but there is no formula, and we must seek the anomalies and clues which can provoke the unique power of human creativity to generate new hypotheses (existing outside the current framework) in pursuit of a new discovery of principle.

What follows are a series of articles elaborating various aspects of this investigation, brought together in pursuit of convergence on a new principle.

energetic, shining more brightly than the entire rest of the galaxy (i.e. producing more energetic output than billions of stars combined). Moreover, evidence indicates this immense activity is coming from an incredibly small region of the galaxy. There are attempts to explain this energetic output from within the current paradigm, but they are very sketchy and contradict observational evidence.

Is it a coincidence that the most energetic phenomenon presently observed in the known Universe is associated with a phenomenon for which our current mathematical framework literally breaks down? Perhaps the energetic output of this mysterious phenomenon is an expression of a new type of reaction, associated with a galactic-level of science (see "Singularities and Supermassive Black Holes," in this report).

In Search of Principle

This is a brief overview of some important lines of investigation into the science of our Galaxy. On the one side, we can study the history of changes on the Earth (and on other bodies in the Solar System) as possible records indicating what the Galaxy is by what it does to lower-order stellar systems. On the other side, we have anomalous features of the large-scale structure and dynamics of a galactic system as a whole, which might

NASA

A Hubble Space Telescope photograph shows a massive jet of plasma being ejected from the massive galaxy M87.

II. Climate Change as a Case Study: Categories of Causality

by Benjamin Deniston

Adapted from a May 14, 2015 research memo

This is a brief examination of the distinction between the different cosmic principles shaping our Earth's climate, water, and weather systems. Other studies has demonstrated that the Sun and the Galaxy act to shape these processes on Earth,[16] but here we will step back and investigate the categorical structure of causality. What is the hierarchy of active principles, and what are the successive boundaries of their respective expressions?

As cited in the opening article to this report, Cusa initiated the needed framework of scientific

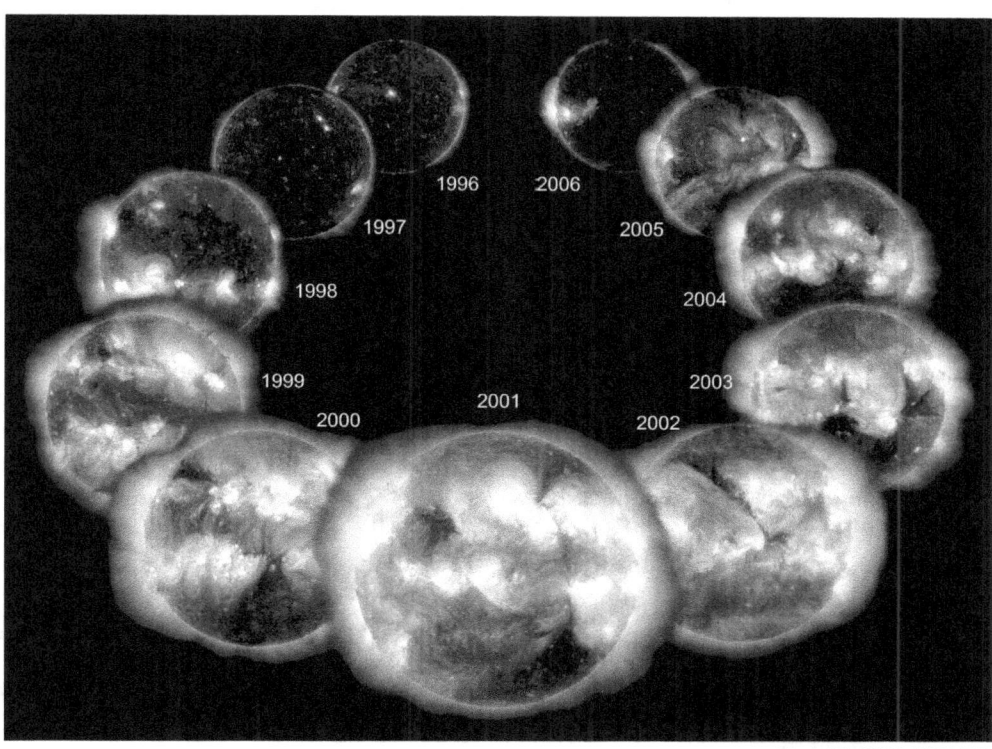

Steele Hill, SOHO, NASA/ESA

Year by year X-ray images of the Sun as it progresses through an eleven year cycle (starting weak in 1996, peaking in 2001, and ending weak in 2006).

thought for this top-down investigation. Another, more recent reference point in this approach is the thesis developed in the November 2014 article, "Time for a Solar Noösphere".[17]

In short: space, time, and material substance—as modern science tends to understand them from an epistemologically sense-perceptual basis—are varying shadows, cast by the actions of principles. As developed in "Time for a Solar Noösphere," we can associate certain boundaries in the scales of temporal, spacial,

energetic, and material action associated with certain principles—and perhaps most importantly, we can define coherence in an anti-sense-perceptual unification of seemingly separate boundaries in the very small and the very short, with boundaries in the very large and the very long.

But these interconnected boundaries—appearing in the shadows of temporal, spacial, energetic, and material expressions—are the effects, not the cause.

Starting from the discoveries of Cusa enables the delusional conceptions of self-defined objects floating in empty space through absolute time to fall away, and provides, instead, a conception of the hierarchical nesting of supra-sense-perceptual principles of development, expressing their distinction (subjugation or sub-

---

16. See the LaRouche PAC show, A New Paradigm for Mankind, for May 6, 2015; also published in *EIR*, May 15, 2015 ("Galactic Man: Shadow versus Principle").

17. November 28, 2014 issue of *EIR*; and LaRouche PAC.

summation) in the effects cast as the boundaries in the scale of spacial and temporal actions.

Climate as a Case Study

With respect to astronomical drivers of the changing climate on Earth, we can define three successive categories of causality—defined by their different strength of influence and by the timescale associated with each process.

Solar Variations—Cycles in solar activity spanning decades to centuries dominate climate variations over scales of thousands of years.[18] However, these variations are subsumed by more influential activity.

Solar System Variations—For the past hundreds of thousands to millions of years, climate change was dominated by variations in the structure of the Solar System (rather than just the Sun alone). Cyclical variations in the Earth's orbital elements and the tilt in the Earth's axis (with periods measured in tens of thousands of years) give rise to the phenomenon referred to as the Milankovitch cycles.[19]

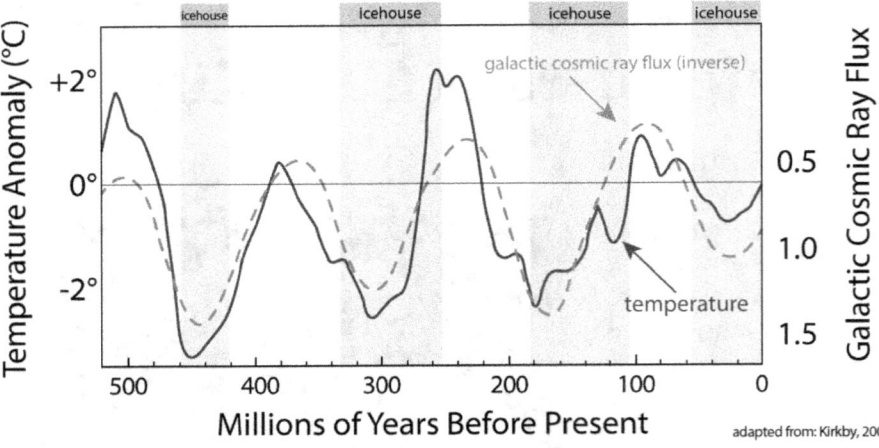

GALACTIC COSMIC RAY FLUX AND TEMPERATURE

galactic cosmic ray flux (inverse)

temperature

Temperature Anomaly (°C)

Galactic Cosmic Ray Flux

Millions of Years Before Present

adapted from: Kirkby, 2008
LaRouche PAC

Spiral Arms, GCR, and Ice Ages.

Galactic Variations—The travels of our Solar System through the Galaxy are measured in tens and hundreds of millions of years. Passages into and out of the Galaxy's spiral arms (approximately every 140 million years) are thought to govern the largest climate changes measured over this time, the major swings from ice house to hot house modes over the past hundreds of millions of years.[20]

This general framework indicates a hierarchical ordering of causality for cosmic drivers of the Earth's climate—the activity of the Sun (alone), subsumed by the activity of the Solar System (as an entirety), subsumed by the activity of the Galaxy. Each lower level is overtaken, in timescale and in the strength of influence, by the higher-order system.

This case study points to the dominating role of the Galactic System (that from which the Solar System was formed and created), providing an important reference point for considerations of causality in the following articles in this report on the galactic principle.

---

18. For example, see the presentation by Professor Carl-Otto Weiss, "Climate Change Is Due To Natural Cycles," at the June 2015 international conference of the Schiller Institute, held in Paris, France.

19. An interesting anomaly arises here—one which could require a return to Kepler's work on the harmonic organization of the Solar System. According to the basic idea of the Milankovitch cycles, different variations in the Earth's orbit (and tilt and precession) change the amount of Sunlight hitting the Earth (and at which times and which locations). It is generally accepted that the periodicities in these orbital variations match climate variations quite well (over the past three million years).

However, when scientists calculate the variation in incident Sunlight which would be caused by these orbital variations they run into a paradox. The factors which are expected by the calculations to have the largest effect on climate, are the changes in the tilt of the Earth and the precession of the equinox, which are cycles of 41,000 and 26,000 years, respectively. But, in the climate records for the past one million years the strongest cycle is neither of these, it is 100,000 years, which corresponds to the changes in the eccentricity of the Earth's orbit.

This is a paradox, since the variation in the amount of Sunlight reaching the Earth attributable to orbital eccentricity changes—according to the referenced calculations—should not be enough to drive the amount of climate variation which is observed in these 100,000 year cycles. Yet the strongest climate variations correspond with the eccentricity

changes, not the tilt or precession changes (for the past one million years). This is referred to as the "100,000-year problem."

This anomaly becomes quite interesting when seen from standpoint of Kepler's work, because the eccentricity is the key factor in Kepler's harmonic hypothesis, and, by his investigation, is connected to the organization of the entire Solar System as a unity. This points in an interesting direction; perhaps the climate variations are a response to changes in the harmonic organization of the entire system (rather than just solar irradiance).

20. "Celestial driver of Phanerozoic climate?" Nir Shaviv and Ján Veizer, GSA Today, July 2003.

III. Solar System Weather Changes Challenge Conventional Theories

by Meghan Rouillard

It is not only on our own planet Earth where we have much to learn about what factors are driving the weather. All around our Solar System, changes are occurring which point toward the need to improve our understanding of Solar System weather as a unified process and study, and the role that solar, galactic, and other factors might be playing.

It is also in examining weather on other bodies in our Solar System that we can easily dismiss assertions that the mere fact that weather on Earth is "changing" is an automatic sign of the massive role that man (and technological progress) must be playing to cause this.

Planet Earth is the only planet currently burdened by a species which, on the whole, has a lot of assumptions about what is, or is not, causing its weather. But the case continues to build for the role which galactic cosmic rays are playing in affecting cloud cover, precipitation, and climate on Earth. Studies have demonstrated the likely presence of this effect at many different time scales— from global ice houses events which corresponds to Earth's passage through the spiral arms of our Galaxy, to changes which seem to mirror solar cycle activity, and even much shorter term changes caused by geomagnetic storms. While these effects appear to vary region by region, and to have different relatively localized expressions, the evidence continues to grow.

Changing Martian Climate

About 10 years ago, the deafeningly stupid, lying campaign of Al Gore, on behalf of truly evil forces who have made no secret of their desire to depopulate (notably Prince Philip), worked many into a frenzy, convinced that man's actual progress was destroying the planet. Many of Gore's forecasts completely failed to pan out. For him, the solar and galactic factors likely driving climate are the real "inconvenient truth!"

While the status of ice caps and glaciers on Earth is far from meeting Al Gore's assertion that, for example, by 2013 the Arctic would be ice-free, Earth is not the only planet which has changes in its surface ice. Take

Mars. Some people have put this forth as a quick example in an attempt to silence those who refuse to think on the matter of climate change. This takes the form of "Ice caps are melting on a planet without human life, so please shut up " As an individual case, it is not really a proof of anything—and with minimal overall ice melting on Earth, trying to show that both planets have global warming is really beside the point. But some of the specifics, and the response to them, were certainly revealing.

In 2005, the Mars Global Surveyor and Odyssey missions showed three years of melting of Mars' southern ice caps prompting debate about what causes climate change on Mars and other planets which don't have human life, and not surprisingly, this evidence was cited frequently during 2007, in the midst of and likely in response to Gore's big campaign. Early indications of the melting prompted some to say that it was simply seasonal and a local change "with no sign of external forcing," but as it continued for three years, reports then focused on the fact that it is no secret that many of Mars' temperature changes are due to changes in Mars' own Milankovitch cycles, which also affect Earth's climate, as changes in orbital characteristics and the planet's wobble and tilt affect its relationship to the Sun.

But these reports usually claimed that this was "well studied" (ironically, these non-anthropogenic cycles are not often discussed with reference to Earth, but this case made it unavoidable). Scientists who posited that changes in solar irradiance could be a factor were generally dismissed for not holding the majority opinion. Essentially, it was claimed that nothing happening on Mars was a surprise. If only that were the only example!

Stormy Planets

There are other changes on Mars and elsewhere in the Solar System which reveal how much more we have to learn about weather and the forces that control it.

Mars is known for some storms, mostly in the form of "dust devils," but recent plumes seen on Mars baffled astronomers. In 2012, several massive plumes were

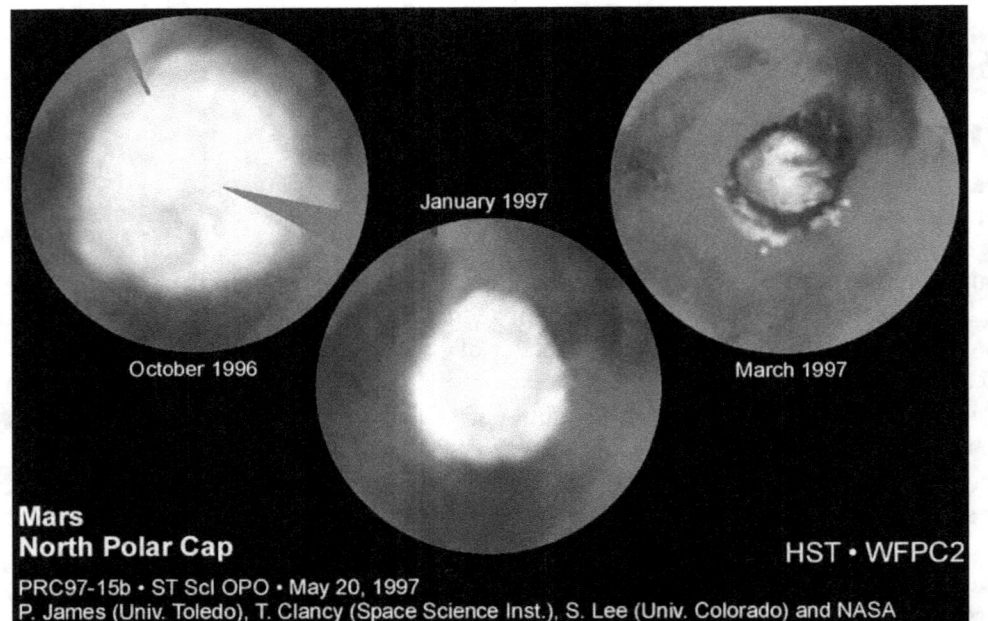

**Mars
North Polar Cap**

January 1997

October 1996

March 1997

HST • WFPC2

PRC97-15b • ST ScI OPO • May 20, 1997.
P. James (Univ. Toledo), T. Clancy (Space Science Inst.), S. Lee (Univ. Colorado) and NASA

P. James (Univ. Toledo), T. Clancy (Space Science Inst.), S. Lee (Univ. Colorado), and NASA. May 20, 1997.

Melting Martian ice caps: "Here a progressive shrinking of one of the Martian polar ice caps is very visible. While this fact should give pause to those who equate melting ice caps with human activity, there is much more to be discovered about the dynamic weather across our solar system."

visible and larger than anything previously observed. Dust has never been seen at comparable altitudes, up to 155 miles above the surface. Two of the explanations put forward, that the plumes were carbon dioxide ice particles or auroral activity, also didn't quite work. Mars' magnetic activity would be too weak for such auroral activity, and its atmosphere should not be cold enough for ice particles to exist at that level. Studies published in *Nature* magazine stated that the plumes seem to defy our current understanding of atmospheric physics on the red planet.

Almost every planet in our Solar System has storms,

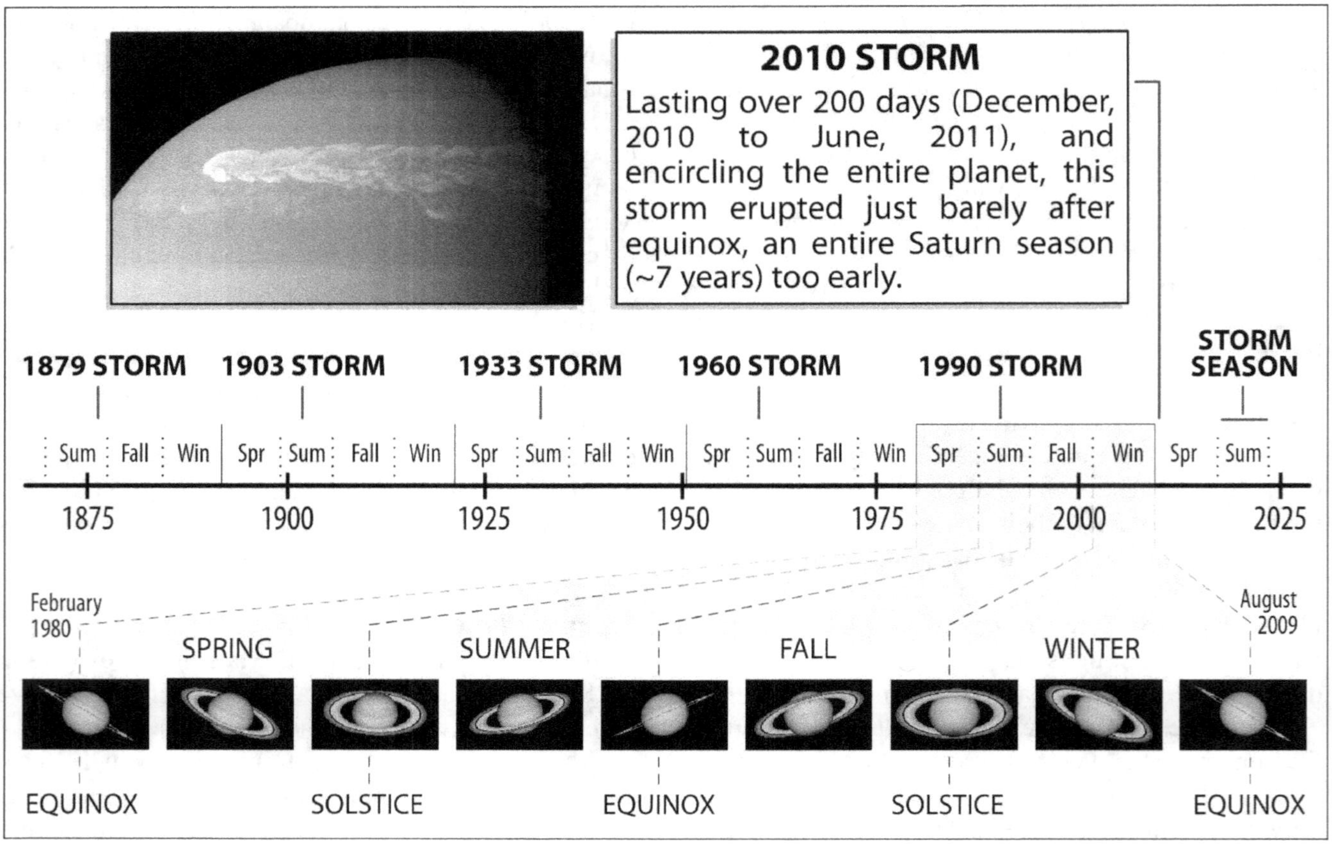

2010 STORM

Lasting over 200 days (December, 2010 to June, 2011), and encircling the entire planet, this storm erupted just barely after equinox, an entire Saturn season (~7 years) too early.

1879 STORM	**1903 STORM**	**1933 STORM**	**1960 STORM**	**1990 STORM**	**STORM SEASON**

	Sum	Fall	Win	Spr	Sum	Fall	Win	Spr	Sum	Fall	Win	Spr	Sum	Fall	Win	Spr	Sum	Fall	Win	Spr	Sum

1875   1900   1925   1950   1975   2000   2025

February 1980

August 2009

SPRING   SUMMER   FALL   WINTER

EQUINOX   SOLSTICE   EQUINOX   SOLSTICE   EQUINOX

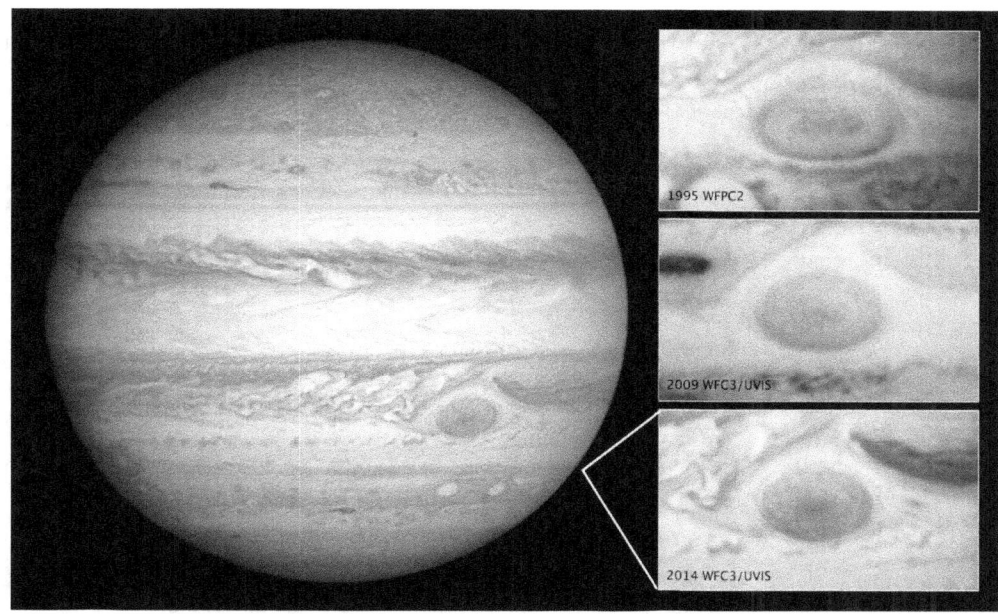

NASA

Jupiter's shrinking spot: "The accelerated shrinking of Jupiter's Great Red Spot currently lacks any clear explanation."

sphere is known to rotate relatively quickly around the planet, compared to its year. Its winds now appear to be rapidly speeding up, clocking in at 300 km/h in 2006 and 400 km/h by 2013. This large variation is new, and has not been observed before, nor is it understood.

Other unprecedented and unexplained changes literally surround us. Jupiter's famous "Great Red Spot" has becomes less intense, and surprisingly so. We have observed this storm for 150 years, but it is now smaller than ever, less than half the size we originally ob-

and storms which change in ways we don't expect. Extraterrestrial vortices are apparent on every planet but Mercury, and even some moons. Venus has such storms as relatively permanent fixtures at each pole, discovered in 2006 by the Venus Express probe. Venus' atmo-

served. While some note that eddies surrounding the storm appear to be changing it, or hypothesize something within the planet's atmosphere that is serving to drain energy from the storm, nothing is certain, and the shrinking appears to be accelerating.

Other storms are picking up in intensity, or simply arriving early based on our understanding of seasons. This was the case for Saturn's last storm. Saturn's seasonal storms have tended to arrive on time like clockwork in the Saturn spring (roughly every 29) years since we began observing in 1876, but this storm arrived quite early—seven years early, to be specific, or an entire season, and it was the largest storm we had ever seen on Saturn. There is also the fascinating case of "Saturn's hexagon," a persisting hexagonal cloud pattern at its North Pole. Attempts to simulate such a formation in the laboratory, by rotating a circular tank of liquid at different speeds between its center and surface, sometimes yielded this shape, but not always.

Studies of the Saturnian moon Titan point towards a solar, and solar-magnetic, influence upon planetary and satellite atmospheres, even at this far distance from it. In a recent paper submitted to the American Geophysical Union entitled "Observed Decline in Titan's thermospheric methane due to solar cycle drivers," the authors put forward evidence of an 11-year cycle, corresponding to the Sun's own 11-year change from

Benjamin Deniston, LaRouche PAC

Saturn' early storm: "As this infographic shows, Saturn's recent "seasonal" storm was anything but seasonal."

solar minimum to solar maximum (corresponding with the intensity of its magnetic activity).

Titan is the only moon in our Solar System with an atmosphere as thick as Earth's. Changes in its atmosphere's chemical makeup, specifically the methane component, is seen to vary according to this cycle, with its methane levels declining with the Sun's activity, and increasing with its inactivity. The authors believe that the radiation expelled from the Sun during flares and other eruptions is actually capable of reaching Titan and breaking apart the methane molecules, a process which was evident during the 2008-2013 period, with methane levels declining as the Sun reached its maximum. This analysis, based on reviewing data from Cassini, also corresponds to the earlier 1980 observations of Voyager, which coincided with a solar maximum and low levels of methane.

The Forgotten Ice Giants

The windy worlds of Uranus and Neptune, with top wind speeds of 560 and 1500 mph respectively, also present paradoxes. These winds are thought to originate due to causes that are either very deep, or, alternatively, very shallow processes in their atmospheres. The fact that the body which is farthest away from the Sun has some of the most intense weather in the Solar System does not have an obvious explanation. In a 2014 BBC documentary on the Ice Giants (part of a series called "The Sky At Night"), planetary scientist Leigh Fletcher of the University of Oxford said the following of these mysterious bodies, which he believes are well worthy of new missions:

> If you look at Uranus and Neptune, they formed at roughly the same sort of temperature, they took about the same length of time to form, you would expect them to be roughly the same. The same sort of composition, the same sort of weather, they have similar colors and that's because of the amount of methane they have in their atmospheres...
>
> But that's where the similarities really end. In fact, Neptune, despite being the farthest planet from the Sun, is actually one of the most dynamic places in our Solar System. It has these incredibly strong weather patterns and weather systems with clouds popping up and large cumu-

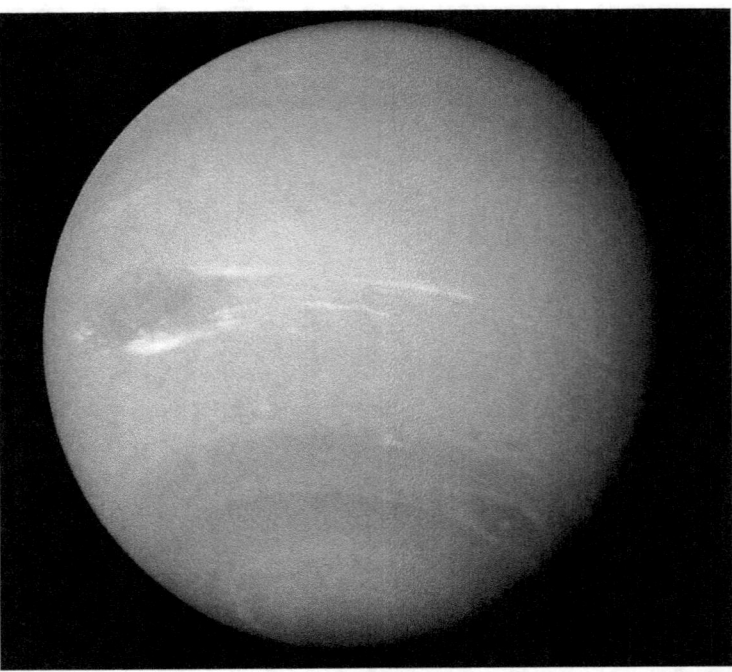

NASA, ESA, and L. Sromovsky (University of Wisconsin)

Neptune spots: "In this image, the two visible spots represent storm activity on Neptune, one of the most distant and most active bodies in our Solar System."

lus systems developing that then get sheared apart by all the winds and jets and these can happen on an hourly basis, so that Neptune really doesn't look the same each night that we look.

> Now contrast that with somewhere like Uranus. Uranus, when Voyager flew past it in the 80's, was a very sluggish, dare I say boring planet. All said and done, Neptune is a much more powerful, much more active planet than Uranus despite being much much farther away at 30 AU vs 20. [The expectation is that this would make the weather less "dynamic."] Most of the giant planets, if you were to look at them with infrared eyes, would be glowing hot, they are emitting energy. Neptune has the biggest heat source of any of the giant planets... maybe that's contributing to this really powerful weather we see on that planet. But then contrast that with somewhere like Uranus. Uranus has almost no appreciable heat source that we can detect.

Fletcher supports a new mission to Uranus to answer some of these questions. But with winds upwards of 500 miles per hour, it can't really be fairly described as

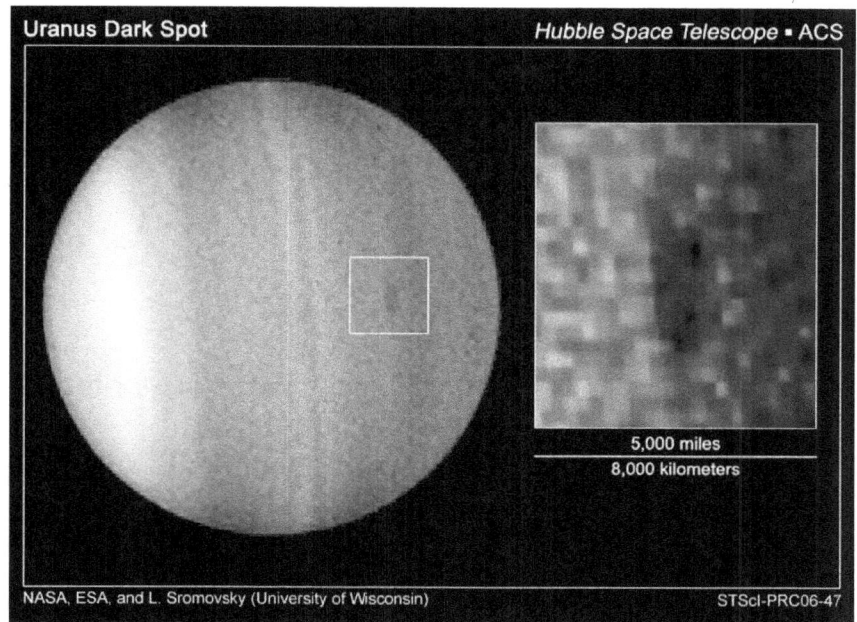

Uranus Dark Spot — Hubble Space Telescope ▪ ACS

5,000 miles
8,000 kilometers

NASA, ESA, and L. Sromovsky (University of Wisconsin)

STScI-PRC06-47

NASA, ESA, and L. Sromovsky (University of Wisconsin)

Uranus Dark spot: "The first image of a dark spot on Uranus, which often appears calm and opaque, obtained in 2006."

boring, and it, like Saturn, has also recently shown evidence of surprising storms.

Uranus' virtual 90 degree tilt to the rest of the planets in our system makes it quite unconventional (and the cause of this tilt in and of itself is an interesting question), but theoretically it could have seasonal weather. In part, it simply hasn't been observed very much or very closely, but there was an increase in reported observations of cloudy spots in 2014, which turned out to be intense storms, viewed by the Hubble Telescope and from the Keck Observatory in Hawaii, with the initial observations drawing attention to it. This activity came seven years after the Northern Spring Equinox of 2007, when each pole was equally illuminated, and which was expected to be the height of convective activity.

The 2014 storms came from the Northern polar region, which, however, should not have sufficiently warmed after its long winter to produce such intense storms. "Why we see these incredible storms now is beyond anybody's guess," said Heidi Hammel of the Association of Universities for Research in Astronomy, and a co-investigator in these recent studies. "These unexpected observations remind us keenly of how little we understand about atmospheric dynamics in outer planet atmospheres," the authors wrote in their paper.

Interplanetary Comparative Cosmoclimatology

All this should be taken as a reminder that we should hesitate before boldly proclaiming that we understand the causes of weather on our own planet. Will we make more progress in our study of weather, and increase the accuracy of our forecasts, if we stop studying each body in our Solar System as a totally unique and distinct place? Should we approach weather in a more systemic way, taking into account the respective differences of each planet, but always the fact that they all interact with our changing Sun and galactic environment?

Of course we shouldn't expect that all the answers we would desire are just a question of analyzing existing data, although there might be interesting discoveries awaiting us there. We should design new missions which seek to answer questions about the role which cosmic radiation might play in driving Solar System-wide weather, as well as comparing cycles in seismicity and volcanism, considerations which have been factored into an upcoming Mars mission called Insight.

Initial comparisons of Earth and recent lunar volcanism appear to show intense activity at roughly the same time. Simply a coincidence? We can reasonably start from the hypothesis that as part of a Solar System, the Sun and its changes may very well play a critical role in all planetary weather, with differences in composition, distance, and other factors determining the magnitude of that effect and its expression.

Let's not close our minds to the possibilities of the science of weather forecasting at this Solar System and even galactic level—it would be a tragedy to block out the study of these forces in the name of blind ideological promotion of the theory of anthropogenic global warming, of which there is scant legitimate evidence at best (not to mention that many promoters of this theory simply view it as a means to encourage depopulation). Let's create a new science—Interplanetary Comparative Cosmoclimatology—the means by which we will improve our weather forecasts, and beyond.

IV. Earth-Moon Comparative Planetology

by Benjamin Deniston

May 31, 2015

As the Solar System has traveled through our Galaxy, it has experienced different galactic environments: the regions north or south of the galactic plane, the central regions of the galactic plane, the spiral arms, various giant molecular clouds, star forming regions, open clusters, etc.

Since evidence is now accumulating to show that different planetary bodies in the Solar System respond (sometimes differently) to these various galactic environments, an examination of the historical experience recorded on (or in) these different bodies can tell us about the Galaxy. Perhaps most interesting are prospective cross-comparisons of the histories of different bodies, looking for indications of when they show certain changes or activity at the same time—indicating they could be responding to the same external influence.

Image Credit:"Eruption chronology of the Columbia River Basalt Group," by T.L. Barry, et al. 2013 Geological Society of America. *This map shows the main regions of flood basalt exposure, resulting from massive lava flows starting sixteen and a half million years ago.*

Cases of weather and climate changes on various planetary bodies were examined in the earlier article.[21] Another example is provided by a 2002 study by Nir Shaviv, "The spiral structure of the Milky Way, cosmic rays, and ice age epochs on Earth," which demonstrates a singleness of convergence from three different paths of investigation.

Path one: Shaviv examined existing models of the motion of our Solar System through the Galaxy, identifying when those models said the Solar System should be passing through the Galaxy's spiral arms.

Path two: Shaviv examined records of major global glaciation events in the Phanerozoic history of the Earth's climate, identifying their periods.

Path three: Shaviv examined iron meteorites, which—before falling to Earth—spent the past hundreds of millions of years orbiting the Sun in interplanetary space, experiencing the changing galactic cosmic radiation conditions of interplanetary space.

The three independent lines of investigation came together to indicate aspects of a single overall picture. On the one side, we have indications of when the whole Solar System may have experienced different galactic

---

21. "Solar System Weather Changes Challenge Conventional Theories," by Meghan Rouillard, in Part III in this report.

The eruption of the Baroarbunga Volcano on September 4th 2014.

Peter Hartree (Attribution-ShareAlike 2.0 Generic)

environments, and, on the other side, we have records of different bodies of the Solar System responding in their own way to changing cosmic environmental conditions (for the Earth, a response of the climate system; for the asteroid pieces which are to become meteorites, a response in the records of chemical transmutation— through galactic cosmic ray spallation—and the subsequent records told by the radioactive decay of the created elements).

For the response of Earth systems, additional examples (besides climate response) include the potential reaction of life and the biosphere to these varying galactic environments.[22]

Here we will briefly focus on provocative evidence indicating that perhaps records of another type of planetary activity might also be telling us about different galactic environments: the processes underlying large-scale planetary volcanic events and geophysical activity more generally.

While such a relation—showing planetary geophysical activity to be responsive to galactic influences— would be extremely challenging to the current paradigm of stellar-level science, this is not the first time the question has been posed. Here, in addition to identifying existing investigations, we will add another bit of evidence, which, to this author's knowledge, hasn't been posed before: the temporal correspondence between the largest three recent periods of lunar volcanism with the last three major periods of flood basalt events on Earth.[23]

Since the geophysical (or comparable) activity within planetary bodies is currently believed to be an isolated and self-determined product of that planetary body, indications for responses to external influences could point to mechanisms associated with a new galactic-level of science.

Biodiversity, Geophysical, and Galactic Cycles

In 2005 a ~60 million year cycle in marine fossil biodiversity was discovered.[24]

Subsequent investigations into the possible cause of this cycle noted that the period and phase of the cycle correspond very well with the modeled motion of our Solar System above and below the plane of our Galactic System.[25] However, a galactic influence guiding the evolution of life has remained outside the scope of thought of most researchers, because it would require the relation (mechanism) to be expressed though a north-south dissymmetrical characteristic in the Galactic System.[26]

22. See "A Vernadskian Reconsideration of Galactic Cycles and Evolution" in this report.

23. Flood basalt events are produced when a massive volcanic eruption or a series of eruptions cover large areas with lava. These can also produce structures called large igneous provinces.

24. "Cycles in fossil diversity," Rohde, Muller; 2005.

25. "Do extragalactic cosmic rays induce cycles in fossil diversity?" Medvedev and Melott, 2007.

26. "A Vernadskian Reconsideration of Galactic Cycles and Evolution," Benjamin Deniston; *EIR*, May 22, 2015.

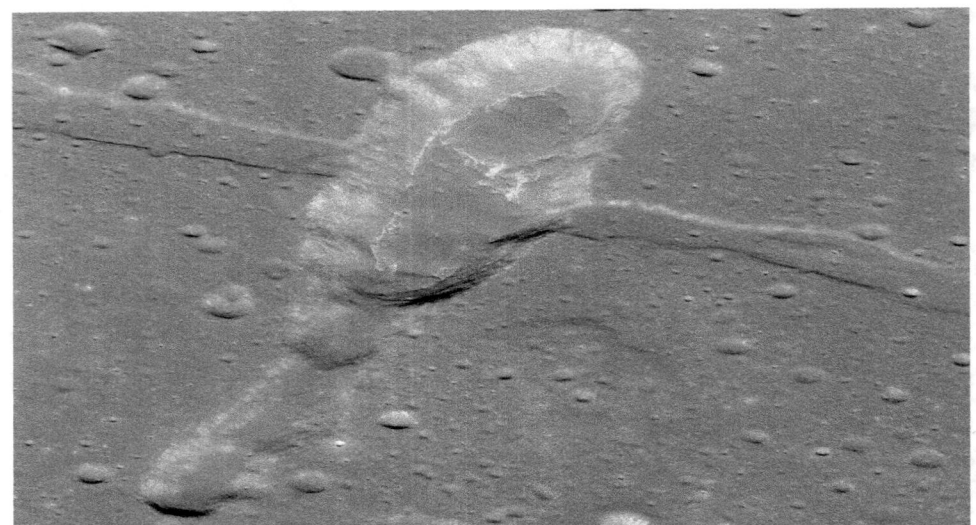
NASA/GSFC/Arizona State University

The Sosigenes lava flow (irregular mare patch) might be just 18 million years old.

approach[30]—examines such correlations between activity of the lower order system associated with its changing relations to the higher-order system as clues and anomalies which might force the need for a new level of science—a new understanding associated with a higher-order galactic principle (and a corresponding higher-order physics, subsuming present notions).

Corresponding independent responses from different planetary bodies in our Solar System (the Earth and Moon) provide an impetus to force more attention to this second approach.

A Cusian Approach

In late 2014 a study was published showing that the Moon has been volcanically active much more recently than scientists had thought.[31]

While it was thought that volcanism on the Moon ended around a billion years ago, this study showed that multiple lunar volcanic structures are almost certainly less than 100 million years old. The study provided approximate dates for the three largest of these recent structures.

•"Sosigenes irregular mare patch" (IMP), covering 4.5 km², is dated to about 18 million years (Myr) ago (+/- 1 Myr)

•"Ina," covering 1.7 km², is dated to about 33 Myr (+/- 2 Myr)

•"Cauchy-5 IMP," covering 1.3 km², is dated to about 58 Myr (+/- 4 Myr)

In pursuit of a Cusian approach, this author thought to compare these three dates with periods of increased volcanic activity on Earth.

Two sources provide the approximate dates for periods of increased large-scale Earth volcanism (referred

At around the same time other studies showed that cycles in geophysical activity (large scale volcanism, sedimentation, and continental uplift) match this ~60 million year biodiversity cycle quite well.[27]

Could the biodiversity cycles and the geophysical cycles both be expressing a response to the changing galactic environment experienced by the Solar System?

There are two ways this question can be approached.

One approach—which could be called the 1900 approach[28]—states that a mechanism must first be posited to explain how the interaction could occur within the framework of currently known (or possibly accepted) physics, and only then can the question be asked. At least one published study (known to this author) has attempted to related biodiversity cycles, geophysical activity, and the motion of our Solar System through the Galaxy in this way; however their mechanism is unable to account for all the correlations between galactic travels and geophysical activity on Earth.[29]

Another approach—what could be called a Cusian

27. "Sixty-two million year cycle in biodiversity and associated geological processes," Rohde, 2006. "60-Myr Periodicity Is Common to Marine Sr, Fossil Biodiversity, and Large-Scale Sedimentation: What Does the Periodicity Reflect?" Melott, Bambach, Petersen, McArthur, 2012.

28. See Jason Ross's presentation to the May 16, 2015 Schiller Institute New York City conference, and "The Escape from Hilbert's 'ZETA' 'X': Mapping the Cosmos!" by Lyndon LaRouche, *EIR*, March 19, 2010.

29. "Disc dark matter in the Galaxy and potential cycles of extraterrestrial impacts, mass extinctions and geological events," Rampino, 2015.

30. *De Docta Ignorantia*, Nicholas of Cusa, 1440.

31. "Evidence for basaltic volcanism on the Moon within the past 100 million years," Braden, Stopar, Robinson, Lawrence, vander Bogert, Hiesinger, 2014.

to as "flood basalt events" or the creation of "large igneous provinces").[32]

As can be seen in the accompanying table, the correspondence with the recent lunar volcanic events is remarkable.

Earth Flood Basalt Events		Recent Lunar Volcanism	
Columbia River Flood Basalts	15.3-16.6 Myr	Sosigenes IMP	18 (+/- 1) Myr
Ethiopian and Yemen traps	29.5-31 Myr	Ina	33 (+/- 2) Myr
North Atlantic Tertiary Volc. Prov. 2	54-57 Myr	Cauchy-5 IMP	58 (+/- 4) Myr

It is generally assumed that volcanic activity is a product of the internal dynamics of a planetary body acting in isolation from the rest of the Solar System and Galaxy.

Yet here we see evidence of two different bodies coming into activity simultaneously—a temporal correspondence in the three largest recent volcanic events on the Moon, and the three most recent flood basalt events on the Earth—as if both bodies (Earth and Moon) were responding to the same environmental influence. This evidence for coordinated interplanetary activity provides potential support for examining the earlier-mentioned longer-term correlation between cycles in other forms of geophysical activity, and the motion of our Solar System through the Galaxy.

Because we only have three events (and room for improvement in the dating of the lunar events), this points to the importance of developing much more detailed investigations of these and other structures on the Moon (as well as on other bodies, such as Mars, various asteroids, other planets, other moons, etc.), enabling a more thorough comparison of the histories of various components of our Solar System in search of indications of a coordinated response to the higher-order Galactic System.[33] This will be critical to further pursuing this path of investigation of the nature of Galactic System, as expressed in the subsumed activity of the Solar System, and its various components.

32. "On the ages of flood basalt events," Vincent E. Courtillot, Paul R. Renne; 2003. "Time-Series Analysis of Large Igneous Provinces: 3500 Ma to Present" Prokoph, Ernst, Buchan, 2004.

33. Another provocative study, examining a much shorter time scale, showed that moonquakes (measured from 1969 to 1977) preferentially occurred when the Moon was facing a specific sidereal position, prompting the author to ask about a "Possible Extra-Solary-System Cause For Certain Lunar Seismic Events" (Yosio Nakamura and Cliff Frohlich, 2006).

NASA

V. A Vernadskian Reconsideration of Galactic Cycles and Evolution

by Benjamin Deniston

May 20, 2015

The following was originally written as a stand-alone article, but is being republished here as an addition to the present report.

As has been emphasized recently by Lyndon LaRouche and his *Executive Intelligence Review* magazine and LaRouche PAC, to understand climate, weather, and the behavior of water on our planet, we must start by understanding the role of our Galaxy. [34]

Records of the largest climate variations over the past half billion years correspond to changes in the galactic environment experienced by our Solar System—indicating that the Galaxy has the strongest role in determining the climate variations on Earth.[35]

The implications of this can be looked at in two ways.

On the one side, an adherent to the modern school of scientific reductionism may see this as, perhaps, an interesting phenomenon, but one with no general impact on our understanding of the nature and ordering of causality in the Universe.

On the other side, a mind which is not suffering from the debilitating effects of the destruction of science led by David Hilbert and Bertrand Russell[36] (mathematical

Yuri Beletsky, August 2010

One of the European Southern Observatory's telescopes in their Very Large Telescope array uses a laser beam to create an artificial star high in the Earth's atmosphere, allowing the astronomers to correct for atmospheric distortion (utilizing adaptive optics) as they study the central regions of our Milky Way Galaxy.

reductionism) will see this as a clue to defining a new understanding of the hierarchical nature of causality in the Universe—pursuing the conception of science defined by Nicolas of Cusa (as in his 1440 De Docta Ignorantia) and his follower Johannes Kepler.

Here, we will take the opportunity of the publication of the first English translation of Vladimir Vernadsky's 1930 report, "The Study of Life and the New Physics," to examine another clue, again pointing us towards the need for a higher understanding of our Galaxy.[37]

Studies have shown that there are cycles in the evolutionary development of animal life over the past 540 million years on Earth—cycles which correspond in period and in phase to cyclical aspects of the motion of our Solar System through our Galaxy.

This can also be looked at in two ways.

1. In the modern domination of Russellian reductionism, a "kill mechanism" is sought to explain how different galactic environments can accelerate the extinction rate of species and, thereby, imprint records of these cosmic fluctuations in the evolutionary record.

2. For an approach freed from the disease of reductionism, we can instead look to the views of Vernadsky, as presented in his 1930 report, "The Study of Life and the New Physics."

A student of Dmitri Mendeleev, and an avid opponent to the influence of Bertrand Russell on Russian and Soviet science, Vernadsky's hypotheses about life in the Cosmos provide an important basis to investigate the relationship between the changing expression of

34. "New Perspectives on the Western Water Crisis," *EIR*, April 3, 2015; "Galactic Man: Shadow versus Principle," *EIR*, May 15, 2015; and the LaRouche PAC water page.

35. See "Celestial driver of Phanerozoic climate?" Nir Shaviv and Ján Veizer, GSA Today, July 2003.

36. For more on the destructive role of Hilbert and Russell, see Jason Ross's presentation to the May 16, 2015 Schiller Institute New York City conference, and "The Escape from Hilbert's 'ZETA' 'X': Mapping the Cosmos!" by Lyndon LaRouche, *EIR*, March 19, 2010.

37. "The Study of Life and the New Physics," translated by Meghan Rouillard.

life on Earth and the subsuming Galactic System.

This provides another avenue for understanding that which subsumes our Solar System, our Earth, and the processes therein.

Identifying the Important Evidence

Fossil records leave a map of the evolutionary development of complex life on Earth, showing an overall increase in the number of distinct animal species (and more clearly in measures of genera) on the planet over the past 540 million years (as is best recorded in records of ocean life). However, upon this overall increase is imprinted a smaller periodic rise and fall in the number of genera at any given time. Early indications of this go back to the 1980s,[38] but more recent analysis (with a more complete fossil record) has solidified the evidence for a cycle in the decline and increase in the number of genera over time.[39] Perhaps most interestingly, this cycle corresponds with the period and phase of cyclical aspects of the motion of our Solar System through the Milky Way Galaxy.

Existing attempts to explain this correlation between galactic activity and evolution of life rely upon a sequence of domino-like effects resulting from the introduction of a "kill mechanism." They look for ways that cosmic processes might kill off large enough numbers of individual animals (either directly, or by creating certain environmental effects which will do so), which, in turn, could then lead to extinctions of entire species; and, if the killing rate were powerful enough and sustained, then to the extinctions of large numbers of different species, resulting in the extinctions of entire genera, and then families, culminating in a "mass extinction."[40]

FIGURE 1
Marine Fossil Diversity

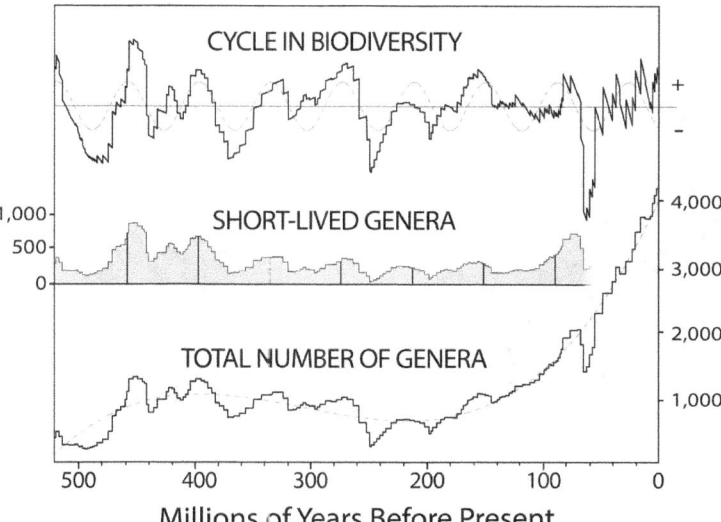

Millions of Years Before Present

adapted from Rohde & Muller, 2005

The belief that increased extinction rates, or even mass extinctions can be explained by this type of a bottom-up causality is not a demonstrated generalization based on evidence, but, rather, the product of certain reductionist beliefs and assumptions. In reality, the phenomena of mass extinctions are still poorly understood.[41] What we know from the fossil record is that there can be relatively rapid—in geological terms—transitions where many species, genera, and families disappear from the record and are replaced by new forms—although these more dramatic (and rapid) shifts exist within the context of an already ongoing slower turnover rate. How and why this occurred the way it did is still not well understood.

So, rather than assuming we must accept a reductionist framework, here we will take a different approach.

Perhaps most important for this shift in approach is

---

38. "Periodic Extinction of Families and Genera," Raup and Sepkoski, 1986, Science, Vol. 231, Issue 4740.

39. "Cycles in fossil diversity," Rohde and Muller, March 10, 2005, Nature, Vol. 434.

40. The initial attempt to define such a kill mechanism posits that high-energy radiation experienced in different parts of the Galaxy damages and kills more animals when the Solar System is in this region, leading to greater extinction rates ("Do extragalactic cosmic rays induce cycles in fossil diversity?" Medvedev and Melott, 2007). In a more recent attempt to explain this correlation, another scientist proposed that the extinctions are the product of comet impacts with the Earth, produced periodically by the Solar System's cyclical passage through more dense regions of the Galaxy (at which times, comets hiding in the outskirts of our Solar System can have their orbits perturbed, sending some towards the inner planets). See, "Disc dark matter in the Galaxy and potential cycles of extraterrestrial impacts, mass extinctions and geological

events," Michael R Rampino, Feb. 18, 2015, Monthly Notices of the Royal Astronomical Society, Vol. 448, Issue 2.

41. For example, a rather thorough 2006 paper by Richard Bambach re-analyzed what is known about extinctions and mass extinctions over the past 540 million years. His last two conclusions were interesting. "Mass extinctions are diverse and vary in intensity, selectivity, and timing. They are not homogeneous in effect or in cause." And, "Knowledge of timing and of geographic and environmental distribution of effects is inadequate. At this time, no consensus on proximate cause of death has been obtained for any extinction event." See, "Phanerozoic Biodiversity Mass Extinctions," Richard K. Bambach, Annual Review of Earth and Planetary Sciences, Vol. 34 (May 2006), pp. 127-155.

Fossilized remains of an extinct species of sea stars (Dipsacaster africanus) from around 130 million years ago. The fossils were discovered in Taba, Morocco.

to recognize that it isn't simply extinctions which define with these cycles, but extinctions and originations (the generation of new species, genera, and families).

As stated in a 2013 paper on the subject by Melott and Bambach, the evidence for a cycle in the process of the evolutionary development of life on Earth "results from the coherent interaction of both extinction and origination fluctuations, producing a stronger signal than either would or could alone."[42] So we must also ask why there exist periodic phases characterized by the origination of new genera.

Put simply, we're looking for more than a kill mechanism. We're examining, on the one side, the anti-entropic development of life on Earth, and, on the other, the relation of our Solar System to our Galactic System—and we're asking why cycles in both processes correlate so well. The work of Vernadsky provides a new basis to investigate this relation, in these top-down terms.

Vernadsky's 'Study of Life and the New Physics'

We don't know what life is.

Vernadsky's work provides an important distinction between the study of living processes and life per se. We can study living processes as effects of life, as par-

ticular expressions of life, without assuming that these specific expressions, alone, define life per se. This important distinction provides the needed framework to properly pursue the properties and characteristics of life, per se—investigating that which underlies certain particular expressions and manifestations.

Vernadsky took up exactly this approach in his 1930 report, "The Study of Life and the New Physics." Examining the identifiable properties of living processes—as they can be studied in the context of their existence in the biogeochemical medium of the Earth's biosphere—he separated the properties into two lists:

> First, those properties which are associated with the planetary (biogeochemical) medium within which living processes are manifested on Earth;
>
> Second, those properties displayed by living processes which can not be attributed to the characteristics and properties of this planetary context, and, thus, might express something more universal about life, per se.[43]

Vernadsky immediately follows this second list with a conclusion which will be upsetting to today's reductionists: "This list is not complete, but it indicates, with evidence, that life manifests itself in the Cosmos in other forms than those which biology normally displays."

Since living processes are not merely a phenomenon of geochemistry[44]—but are an expression of a principle of life, per se, manifested in the context of a geochemical medium—we should be willing to seek out in the Cosmos, other expressions of these non-planetary properties of life.

Vernadsky then dedicates the entire latter half of his report to the two non-planetary properties of life, which he thinks could be the most fruitful in investigating how "life manifests itself in the Cosmos in other forms than those which biology normally displays."

> Here, I will dwell upon two phenomena which will allow for the clarification of the important role which the investigation of life plays in the scientific picture of the Universe, created by the new physics, notably upon the dissymmetry of the space of living organisms and on biological

42. "Analysis of periodicity of extinction using the 2012 geological timescale," Melott and Bambach, 2013; citing, "A ubiquitous ~62-Myr periodic fluctuation superimposed on general trends in fossil biodiversity. II. Evolutionary dynamics associated with periodic fluctuation in marine diversity," Melott and Bambach, 2011, Paleobiology.

43. See section 10 of "The Study of Life and the New Physics." See footnote 37.

44. Despite the delusions of Vernadsky's opponent and adversary, Alexander Oparin. See, "A.I. Oparin: Fraud, Fallacy, or Both?" by Meghan Rouillard, Spring 2013 issue of *21st Century Science & Technology*.

time. In the first case, this is a matter of new properties (a particular state of physical space), observed in living organisms, and in the second, new properties of physical time.[45]

In his 18-section report, Vernadsky focuses most of the latter half to the first of these two, "the dissymmetry of the space of living organisms" (sections 11-16), followed by one section on biological time (section 17).

Vernadsky's work—both distinguishing a principle of life, per se, from the particular expressions of living processes we're familiar with on Earth, and positing the need to investigate other potential expressions of this principle in the Cosmos—provides a critical, non-reductionist basis for investigating the correlation of cycles of extinction and origination in the fossil record with the cycles of our Solar System's motion through our Galaxy—that is, to investigate the potential relationship between the process of the anti-entropic development of living processes on Earth, and the processes of the cosmic system of our Galaxy.

As we will see, Vernadsky's conception of dissymmetrical states of space will be key.

Cosmic Dissymmetry

In a different address (delivered one year later), Vernadsky made some interesting remarks specifically regarding Galactic Systems. Citing early studies examining the distribution of "spiral nebulae" (as spiral galaxies used to be called), Vernadsky hypothesized their orientations could be an expression of a "dissymmetrical" characteristic of the Cosmos.

The spiral form of nebulae and of some stellar agglomerations indicates the probable presence of analogous dissymmetrical phenomena in the Cosmos. If the right spirals predominate in effect, clearly, among the spiral nebulae, as numerous photographs attest, or in certain parts of the Universe, right spiral nebulae are concentrated, and in others left spiral nebulae, the existence of dissymmetric spaces in the Cosmos would become more than probable. This dissymmetry would seem to be analogous to that which we observe in the space penetrated by life, that is to say, that it possesses enantiomorphic vectors and both of the

vectors—left and right—could exist there at the same time, but not in equal number; the right-handed vectors most often predominate there.[46]

While recent studies indicate Vernadsky may have been onto something interesting regarding the large-scale distribution of galaxies,[47] here we're interested in the potential dissymmetrical characteristics of a single Galaxy—our own.

For a single spiral galaxy to express an inherent dissymmetry—i.e., to have an inherent handedness—there has to be a physical distinction between the top and bottom (north and south),[48] a distinction expressing the global characteristics of the galactic system as a whole.

Most importantly, if we are working from Vernadsky's conception of potential cosmic expressions of a quality of dissymmetrical space which we see expressed in living organisms, then perhaps the top-bottom (north-south) distinction which defines the dissymmetry of a spiral galaxy should be expressed in the response of living processes most strongly. That is, it would make sense that the most important evidence for defining an inherently dissymmetrical space of a galaxy would be the reaction of living processes to the influence of that dissymmetrical space.

Holding that thought, let's return to what we know about the relationship of our Solar System to the Galaxy.

As we orbit around the center of our Galaxy, the

45. See section 11 of "The Study of Life and the New Physics." See footnote 37.

46. From Vernadsky's 1931 speech, "On the Conditions of the Appearance of Life on Earth," translated from French by Meghan Rouillard. See footnote 37.

47. Although it is unclear exactly which "spiral nebulae" (spiral galaxies) Vernadsky was referring to in 1931, 80 years later, a professor from the University of Michigan, Michael Longo, published a study showing that there is indeed a preferred orientation to spiral galaxies, depending on which direction one looks. Using a data set of 260,000 clearly defined spiral galaxies, Longo found that in a specific direction (about 10° from the spin axis of our own Galaxy), we see more left-handed spiral galaxies than right-handed ones. In a following study, looking from the Southern Hemisphere (instead of the Northern), Longo showed that, in the exact opposite direction, the opposite is the case: There are more right-handed galaxies are seen than left-handed ones. This is a remarkable finding, one we can be sure Vernadsky would find highly significant. See "Detection of a Dipole in the Handedness of Spiral Galaxies with Redshifts z ~0.04," by Michael J. Longo, Physics Letters B, 699, pp. 224-229 (2011).

48. Otherwise, a spiral galaxy which appears to be right-handed when being observed from one side would, at the same time, appear to be left-handed when observed from the other side. The left vs. right distinction would merely be a product of the location of observation, not an intrinsic expression of the galactic system itself, unless something distinguished one side from the other.

FIGURE 2

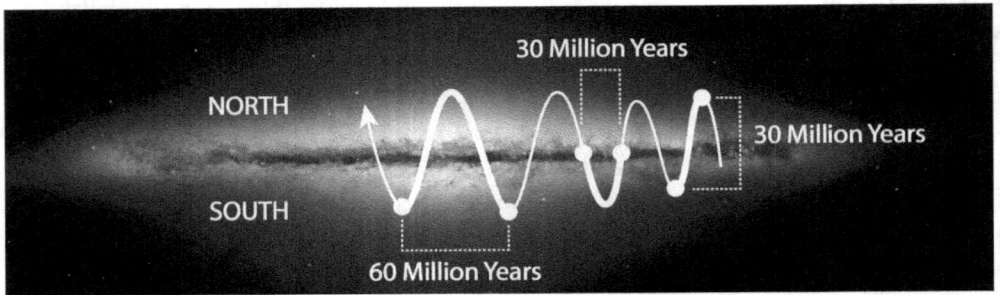

NASA, ESA, & Hubble Heritage Team (STScI/AURA)

Variations in the climate, the temperature, corresponding to the motion of our Solar System, above and below the galactic plane are shown here.

Solar System also passes above and below the galactic plane, in a bobbing-type motion. Based on current measurements and analysis, the cycles of this up-and-down motion are roughly 30 (26-37) million years from mid-plane, through a peak, back to mid-plane, or 30 million years from one peak to the opposite peak, or 60 million years from one peak, through the opposite, and back to the same side. (See Figure 2).

Most researchers think that the conditions north or south of the galactic plane should be generally similar, and, therefore, any imprint of this changing galactic environment recorded in the Earth's history should express a 30-million-year periodicity.

In fact this is true for at least one abiotic process, the climate, where a 30-million-year cycle has been found.[49]

However, records of the evolutionary development of life on Earth display a ~62-million-year fluctuation.[50] As mentioned above, this biodiversity cycle appears strongest when one is not only examining extinctions, but extinctions together with originations (the appearance of new genera), a pairing which forces the investigation beyond the reductionist's search for a kill mechanism.

Thus, the evidence for a relationship between processes of our Galactic System, and the evolutionary development of life on Earth, is not simply associated with being either above or below the galactic plane, but with the characteristics of one side vs. the other. Within the reductionist camp, this is taken as evidence to doubt the existence of a connection between this galactic process and the evolution of living processes on Earth (despite the clear correlation), because the reductionists have no reason to hypothesize a distinction between the north and south sides.[51] But when viewed from the conceptions of Vernadsky, the distinction which serves as their basis for doubt becomes our point of interest.

A physical distinction between one side of the Galaxy and the other is required for our Vernadskian hypothesis of a dissymmetrical characteristic governing the physical space of the Galactic System—providing the critical evidence needed to define a distinct, intrinsic handedness of the system (irrespective of one's vantage point).

The evolutionary cycle being 60 million years, rather than 30 (and matching the proper phase), provides the needed evidence for a distinction, indicating the potential for an inherent difference in the north vs. south sides of our Galaxy, and, thereby, its inherent dissymmetry. It is most appropriate that fluctuations in the history of the evolutionary development of living processes on Earth are what provide the critical evidence for defining an intrinsic dissymmetry of our Galactic System—indicating galactic manifestation of dissymmetrical space, to which living processes on Earth are responsive.[52]

Space-Time of Anti-Entropy

In the terminology and framework pursued by Vernadsky, this could be an expression of a [[the]] dissymmetrical spacetime characteristics of our Galactic System.[53]

49. See "Is the Solar System's Galactic Motion Imprinted in the Phanerozoic Climate?" by Nir Shaviv, Andreas Prokoph, and Ján Veizer; Scientific Reports, Article number: 6150 doi:10.1038/srep06150, published Aug. 21, 2014.

50. Indications of other cycles have also been identified, but this one is clear and unambiguous, as stated in the initial paper identifying its existence, "…the 62-Myr cycle is not a subtle signal. It is evident even in the raw data, dominant in the short-lived genera and strongly confirmed by statistical analysis." See "Cycles in fossil diversity," Rohde and Muller, March 10, 2005, Nature, Vol. 434.

51. For example, "The Sun currently oscillates up and down across the Galactic plane every 52-74 [million years], but plausible responses would seem to occur every mid-plane crossing (namely 26-37Myr)" (Rohde, Muller; "Cycles in fossil diversity," 2005); and "Thus, these ~60 Ma periodicities are probably unrelated to the 32 Ma cycle discussed here, unless there is a very large north-south asymmetry relative to the galactic plane" (Shaviv, Prokoph, Veizer, "Is the Solar System's Galactic Motion Imprinted in the Phanerozoic Climate?" 2014).

52. Recall how Vernadsky was calling for investigating how "life manifests itself in the Cosmos in other forms than those which biology normally displays."

53. Vernadsky often focused on, and returned to the space-time proper-

This is not the first indication that the study of Galactic Systems could require a new conception of a self-bounded space-time intrinsic to that Galactic System.[54] However, Vernadsky's direction of work indicates that we should open our minds to the qualities of the space-time characteristics of living processes (rather than simply abiotic physics), if we are to truly attempt to understand the Cosmos as containing a principle of life, per se, and galactic systems therein.

With this evidence for a relation between the evolutionary development of life on Earth and the processes of our Galactic System, we see the option to invert the investigation—to examine the characteristics expressed by evolution as informing us about the nature of our Galactic System as a whole.

As Vernadsky correctly identified in his 1926 address on evolution,[55] there is an intrinsic direction in the evolutionary development of life on Earth—the increasing energy-flux density of the biosphere system—which Vernadsky called his "second biogeochemical principle":

> This biogeochemical principle which I will call the second biogeochemical principle can be formulated thus: The evolution of species, leading to the creation of new, stable, living forms, must move in the direction of an increasing of the biogenic migration of atoms in the biosphere....

[This second biogeochemical principle] indicates, in my opinion, with an infallible logic, the existence of a determined direction, in the sense of how the processes of evolution must necessarily take place.... All theories of evolution must take into consideration the existence of this determined direction of the process of evolution, which, with the subsequent developments in science, will be able to be numerically evaluated. It seems impossible to me, for several reasons, to speak of evolutionary theories without taking into account the fundamental question of the existence of a determined direction, invariable in the processes of evolution, in the course of all the geological epochs. Taken together, the annals of paleontology do not show the character of a chaotic upheaval, sometimes in one direction, sometimes in another, but of phenomena, for which the development is carried out in a determined manner, always in the same direction, in that of the increasing of consciousness, of thought, and of the creation of forms augmenting the action of life on the ambient environment.[56]

Since Vernadsky's time, we've accumulated a much larger and more detailed map of the evolutionary development of life. While the new evidence strongly conforms to Vernadsky's second biogeochemical principle,[57] we are still far from understanding the principle which has composed that map.

In pursuit of this, we've been pointed to the processes of our own Galactic System—as the macroevolutionary pulsations associated with the anti-entropic development of living processes on Earth beat in harmony with our Solar System's experience of the dissymmetrical characteristics of our Galaxy.

Rather than simply an Earth-based phenomenon, the development of life on Earth could be an expression of an anti-entropic character of our Galaxy, returning us to the opening challenge: understanding the causal role of our Galactic System in the hierarchical ordering of the Universe.

ties of living processes as critical to investigating and understanding life phenomena. He developed the need to consider the space-time of living processes as dissymmetrical with a polar vector. This is the case in the cited paper, "Life and the New Physics" (see footnote 37), as well as other works, emphatically his series on the Problems of Biogeochemistry, available in "150 Years of Vernadsky: The Biosphere," 21st Century Science & Technology, Jason Ross (Editor), Meghan Rouillard (Series Editor).

54. Observational evidence indicating discrepant redshift measurements for galactic systems (i.e., redshift values which cannot be attributed to any currently accepted cause of redshifts, such as cosmological expansion, recessional velocity, or relativistic effects), can (although highly controversial) be taken as possible evidence for unique space-time characteristics distinct to an individual galactic system (see Quasars, Redshifts and Controversies, Halton Arp, 1988, Cambridge University Press). Also the "M-sigma relation" (showing that the mass of a galaxy's bulge scales in a very tight proportion to the mass of a phenomenon often referred to as the supermassive black hole at the center of that same galaxy) indicates a higher structure and coherence to a galactic system as a unity. These (and other provocative lines of evidence) tickle the imagination to ponder the yet-to-be-discovered principle organizing the existence and development of a galactic system.

55. "The Evolution of Species and Living Matter," 1926, translated from French by Meghan Rouillard.

56. This second biogeochemical principle should also be considered as a non-planetary property of life, according to Vernadsky's analysis in his "Study of Life Phenomena and the New Physics." See footnote 37.

57. For example, see, "Macro-Ecological Revolutions: Mass Extinctions as Shadows of Anti-Entropic Growth," Benjamin Deniston, EIR, March 23, 2012.

VI. Singularities and Supermassive Black Holes

by Benjamin Deniston

Adapted from an April 2014 research report

Stepping away from studies of what changes and activity in the Solar System tells us about the Galaxy, we can also look at certain categorical aspects which appear to be features of all galaxies as a class. Here we will focus on a characteristic supermassive phenomenon thought to be at the center of each galaxy, the immense energetic activity associated with that phenomenon, and how the mass properties of that phenomenon are intimately tied to global features of the entire galactic system.

Perhaps we can say that we now look at the phenomenon referred to as "supermassive black holes" as scientists of the early Nineteenth Century looked at the Sun.

Then, in the 1800s, it was clear the Sun had been burning for a very, very long time. But what was it burning to be able to sustain itself for so long? If it was some form of chemical combustion there is no way it could sustain that level of energetic output for hundreds of millions or billions of years! Yet records were showing that advanced life had been sustained for a half billion years by a consistent and vigorous output from our star, and that our star has bathed our planet in its warmth for even much longer. This was a paradox—one unsolvable in the scientific framework of the Nineteenth Century. It took a complete revolution, overturning the fundamental understanding of the scientific nature of the Universe to provide the framework to begin to understand the Sun.

Today, we ask, "what is a supermassive black hole and the associated phenomenon of an active galactic nucleus?"

A Singularity

As was recognized not long after their development, the Einstein field equations of Einstein's general theory of relativity showed that if an object was massive enough and small enough, it would cause the spacetime metrics to run off to infinity—creating a mathematical

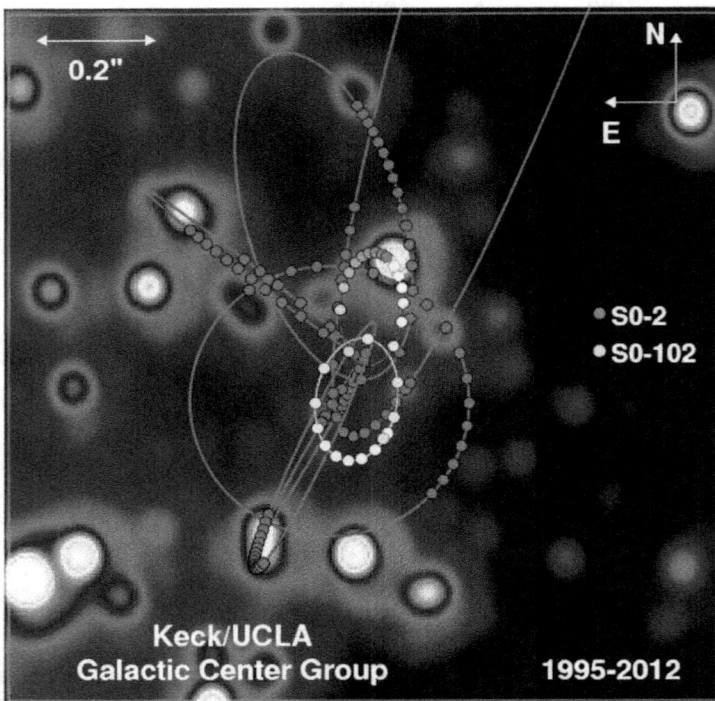

Image 1

Prof. Andrea Ghez and her research team at UCLA; based on data sets obtained with the W. M. Keck Telescopes

The orbits of stars within the central arcsecond of our Galaxy. The orbits have been inferred from images taken with the primitive technique of speckle imaging (1995 - 2005) and with the more sophisticated adaptive optics (2005-2012). While several stars can be seen in their motion through this region, only two stars (S0-2 and the newly discovered S0-102) have been traced through a complete orbit. They are the most tightly bound to the black hole and therefore comprise the most information about it. S0-2, which has an orbital period of 16 years, proved the existence of a black hole. The addition of S0-102, with a period of 11.5 years, will for the first time allow us to test the warping of space and time this close to a black hole.

gravitational spacetime singularity. But what would actually happen here? The equations say as the gravity becomes infinite, time stops, and space becomes unintelligible, but would actually happen in the real Universe? No one knows, as the entire framework of the mathematical physics literally breaks down.

While this was treated as a mathematical construct for years, at some point there arose the actual prospects for the discovery of physical objects massive enough and small enough to meet the mathematical criterion which would supposedly lead to such a singularity. These are generally referred to as black holes.

Theoretically, if a star is large enough, supposedly at the end of its life-cycle, it should be able to collapse on itself with enough force to compress the core to these singularity-generating conditions. Today there are astronomical candidates for such stellar-mass black holes.

However, here we're interested in another type of so-called black hole, a supermassive black hole, like the one at the center of our Galaxy called Sag A*. Being four million times the mass of our own Sun, this couldn't have come from the collapse of a single star, and is part of this other, supermassive, class.[58] Using adaptive optics on the Keck telescope, astronomers have been able to observe entire stars tracing out clean elliptical orbits around a point in space at the very center of our Galaxy where nothing is seen (taking as little as 16 years to do so). This is the most solid observational evidence for the existence of a supermassive black hole (**see Image 1**).

But what is it? What is happening there?

Before considering this question, let us first ask if there are any other places where mathematical singularities arise in the investigation of physical processes, and if these cases, comparing a mathematical infinity with a physical reality, provide any general insight for how to approach such questions?

A useful case might be Riemann's work on the acoustical shockwave.

Long before the advent of supersonic flight, it was calculated that as the speed of sound is approached, the density of sound waves would continuously build up, increasing asymptotically as the speed limit is approached, creating a physical barrier. The mathematical interpretation says the density of sound waves goes to infinity, creating what appeared to be an insurmountable singularity. Yet Riemann was able to forecast that—in physical reality—this barrier could be transcended, a solution that many claimed had some neat

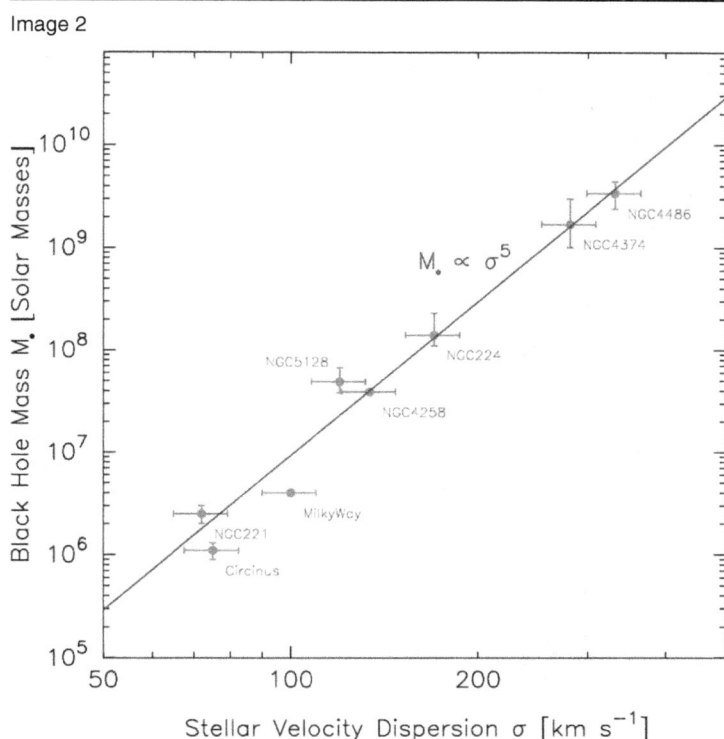

Image 2

Msigma at English Wikipedia

Black hole mass plotted against velocity dispersion of stars in the galaxy bulge [a measure of the mass of the bulge]. Points are labeled by galaxy name; all points in this diagram are for galaxies which exhibit a clear, Keplerian rise in velocity near the center, indicative of the presence of a central mass. The M-sigma relation is shown in blue.

mathematical tricks, but which had no bearing on physics. In reality, exactly the opposite was the case.

Perhaps this provides a conceptual reference point for how to think about the relationship between mathematical singularities in the Einstein field equations, and the observational evidence for something we tend to call "supermassive black holes." The mathematics go to infinity, but that may just signal a phase shift in the physics—in this case, likely a higher-order domain.

Unified Structure

Every galaxy is thought to contain one supermassive black hole in its center. This brings us to a most interesting phenomenon referred to as the "m-Sigma" or black hole-bulge relation (**see Image 2**). This is an empirical observation, showing that the mass of the spherical bulge of a galaxy is always the same proportion greater than the mass of the single supermassive black hole at its center. This holds for smaller galaxies and for larger galaxies.

This is a major challenge to explain in the current

---

58. It is thought every galaxy has a supermassive black hole at its center. It's assumed that a supermassive black hole is produced by the accumulation of many stellar black holes (and other material), but the lack of any black holes in size ranges in-between (so-called intermediate class black holes) poses a challenge to that assumed idea of the origin of supermassive black holes.

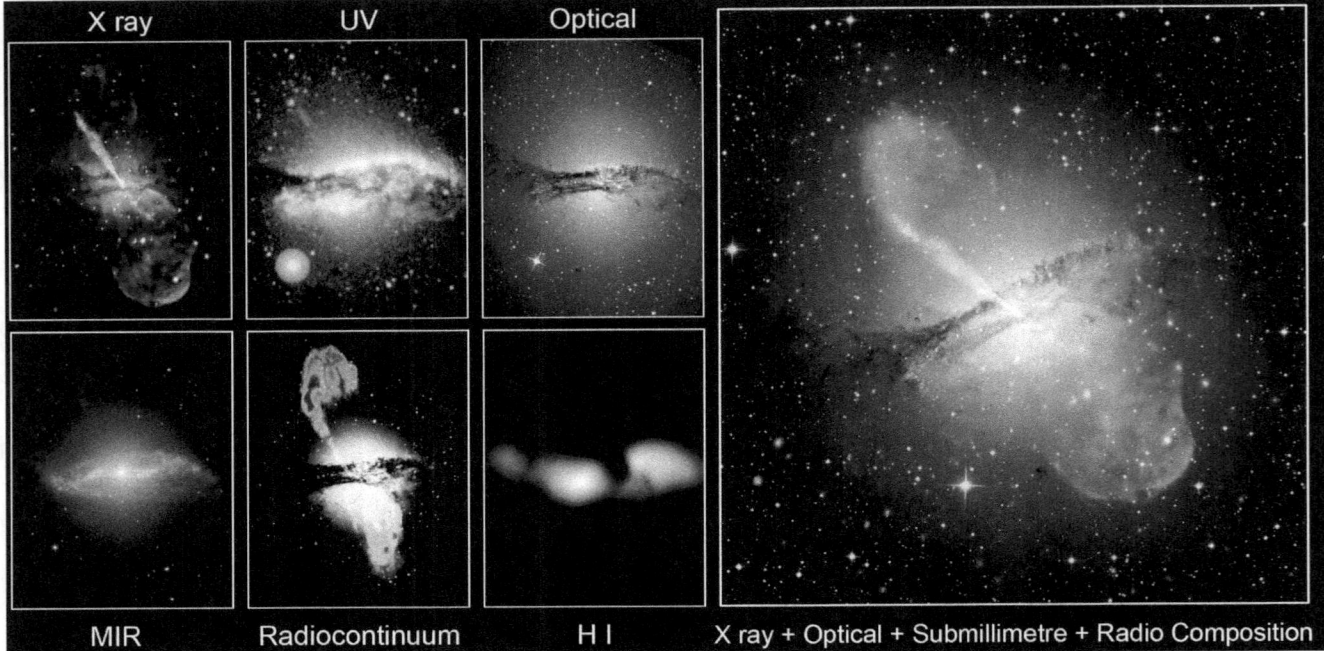

X ray	UV	Optical	
MIR	Radiocontinuum	H I	X ray + Optical + Submillimetre + Radio Composition

Centaurus A is a giant elliptical galaxy - the closest active galaxy to Earth. This remarkable composite view of the galaxy combines image data from the x-ray (Chandra), optical (ESO), radio (VLA) [and more] regimes. Centaurus A's central region is a jumble of gas, dust, and stars in optical light, but both radio and x-ray telescopes trace a remarkable jet of high-energy particles streaming from the galaxy's core. The cosmic particle accelerator's power source is a black hole with about 10 million times the mass of the Sun coincident with the x-ray bright spot at the galaxy's center. Blasting out from the active galactic nucleus toward the upper left, the energetic jet extends about 13,000 light-years. A shorter jet extends from the nucleus in the opposite direction. Other x-ray bright spots in the field are binary star systems with neutron stars or stellar mass black holes.

framework of a stellar-level science. Despite its immense mass, a supermassive black hole should not be able to act to determine the mass of the entirety of the galaxy or its bulge, or vice versa—especially with such consistency.[59]

It would make sense that there is a general relation, with larger galaxies generally having larger supermassive black holes (and vice versa). But the observed proportion between the bulge mass and the supermassive black hole mass is too precise and narrow to find acceptable explanation so far.

It would be comparable to discovering that the height of the largest mountain on every continent is always exactly one five-thousandth of the size of that continent. Or if we noticed that every planet has one moon that is exactly one ten-thousandth the mass of the planet. We might expect some very broad relationships,

but finding anything so precise would be very strange and surprising.

With the supermassive black holes and their host bulge, it is that precise. We can find analogies in the natural world, but only when we look to living (instead of non-living) processes. For example, this galactic scaling relationship is more like how the size of a heart will scale with the size of an animal. That makes sense for animals, because we recognize animals as single entities which grow, develop, and change as a unity. In contrast, the current scientific paradigm assumes the development of galaxies to be a product of the accumulations of actions of individual parts with no single principle governing the whole—an assumption that appears, even from just this evidence, to be false.

What more can we know about this fascinating phenomenon of the supermassive black hole?

Energy Flux Density

Another phenomenon associated with some supermassive black holes is known as "active galactic nuclei." A small percentage of galaxies have extremely

---

59. It is thought that there are some interactions. A host galaxy is thought to provide the material by which its supermassive black hole grows, and it is thought that the energetic output of a supermassive black hole could affect star formation. But why such interactions would produce a tight proportional relationship in the mass is a mystery.

bright and active centers, emitting energy across the electromagnetic spectrum, shining more brightly than the entire surrounding galaxy (containing billions of stars), and sometimes ejecting massive amounts of material out of the galaxy.

These active galactic nuclei are the most energetic (while sustained) phenomenon known in the Universe.

Some active galactic nuclei—such as Centarus A, the closest active galaxy to us—shoot out "jets" or "lobes" of plasma, which can extend well beyond the reach of the galaxy itself (**see Image 3**).

To power such incredible powerhouses of activity, our mysterious supermassive black hole is brought back into the equation. There is simply no source of energy—within the current paradigm of stellar-level science—which can sustain the observed activity of the active galactic nucleus, other than the gravitational singularity.

The current theory is that the immense gravitational attraction of the supermassive black hole pulls gas, dust, stars, etc. into a concentrated spinning disc of material spiraling towards the event horizon (creating an accretion disk), and this pre-event horizon disk of activity is so intense that it radiates energy, jets of material, and everything else that we observe with an active galactic nucleus.

However, this is all theory, and an unstable one at that. A recent study with data from NASA's WISE space telescope appears to overturn key elements of this theory.[60]

Yet we do observe active galactic nuclei, and their jets and lobes, with all their splendor. And we do have observational evidence for something (a so-called supermassive black hole) which appears to approach the criterion of the mathematical singularity, where the current paradigm of mathematical physics breaks down. And we have reason to believe there is a connection between the two—the phenomenon which exists beyond the boundaries of current science, associated with the most energetic activity currently known in the observable Universe.

Prometheus holding Hercules' Galaxy, adapted from "Prometheus Brings Fire to Mankind," by Heinrich Friedrich Fuger, 1817.

A Hypothesis

As the solution to the Nineteenth Century mystery of our Sun depended upon a revolution in our understanding of some of the most fundamental conceptions about the nature of the Universe (matter, energy, space, and time), we must open our minds to the possibility that a similar revolutionary shift will be needed to understand our Galaxy.

The tight relationship between a supermassive black hole and its galaxy provokes considerations of a causality which is not mediated through the available mechanisms provided by the current stellar level of science.

Perhaps these investigations challenging the boundaries of known physics in the very large will equally couple back to the anomalies and limits in the very small.

The unmatched energetic output from a region where current mathematical physics reaches a singularity (breakdown) causes us to wonder about new reactions and processes which could be as outside of our current understanding as was $E=mc^2$ in 1850.

How would such a subsuming physics of the Galaxy subsume and reshape our concepts of energy, space, time, and matter? Of causality? And, perhaps most interesting, what would such a leap bring for mankind?

As the energy density of nuclear reactions leaped orders of magnitude beyond that of chemical reactions, we are left to ponder the capabilities provided to mankind wielding a Galactic Principle.

Somewhere, deep in the Universe, Prometheus awaits our arrival, holding the fire of an active galactic nucleus in hand.

60. "NASA's WISE Findings Poke Hole in Black Hole 'Doughnut' Theory," May 22, 2014.

'We Are Entering a New State of the World Economy With the Four Senators' Reintroduction of Glass-Steagall'

The following is excerpted from the July 11 discussion by Lyndon LaRouche with an audience assembled in Manhattan, New York. The discussion was moderated by Dennis Speed. To see the full video of the dialogue, click here.

Lyndon LaRouche: Right now there is a great change in the destiny of the United States: It's centered in origin or location by a group of four Senators, who have restored as their intention, the relatively immediate reintroduction of the Glass-Steagall law. Now, this has some very special implications: First of all, it means that Wall Street, which is already now bankrupt, but it's sort of hiding from the outcome of its bankruptcy; it's broken down; it's in a freeze state—Wall Street must be removed.

Now, the way we can do that, to save our nation despite the crisis which is threatening us right now,—in other words, Wall Street now threatens to cause a very destructive, sudden force, in the lifestyle of our nation and the people of our nation. This has to be treated in an orderly way, so there are some things I shall not push on this occasion, be-

cause I want to give some of the people in the Congress, especially these four Senators, and some other people who are very relevant, a chance to state what the issue is,—to make a rather simple, but straightforward explanation of what the remedy is and what the problem has been.

So I'll base myself in my remarks today, here, as initial remarks, on that basis. The fact is, therefore, that Wall Street is about to be eliminated. Now I have some ideas and information on exactly what that means, but I'm not going to elaborate those because I would rather let those things be passed back to the Senators, because they are going to have to make certain decisions about

EIRNS/Julien Lemaître

Lyndon LaRouche, at the Schiller Institute conference in Frankfurt, Germany, April 2013, with his wife Helga.

how they approach this motivation. And I will simply make notes on that. I do have a systemic view of what the solution is, to get out of the breakdown of the Wall Street system.

I can assure people that this is seriously understood. It's also understood that the Glass-Steagall system is there, waiting, and that the Wall Street system is in terminal disarray. In other words, it's virtually frozen, with some of its problems hidden for various reasons. But we're entering into a new state of the world economy, because whatever the United States does, as expressed by the active role of those four Senators—and I'm sure they're very intelligent Senators and they know what they're doing—so I'm not going to try to muck up and interfere with what they're going to do. I know in advance, that I'm in support of it, and this will be a solution for the people of the United States and others,

Therefore, I can assure you, that if that program that they have launched is carried through successfully, over opposition, that the United States will come out of this mess, clean and much better than it's been for many years before.

That's my point.

Dialogue

The Fate of Greece

Q: Okay. Hi, Lyn. This is A— from New York. My question is in relation to Greece. One day after the historic victory of the vote, the Finance Minister resigned. And I read earlier on the site to get ready for all types of hell to start breaking loose. So you try and stay calm, but when these things happen, you don't know how to interpret it. What are the implications of such a resignation?

Then of course, just earlier this morning, you get reports on television that, indeed, the Prime Minister has now agreed to some kind of reforms, or cuts. I'm not saying I believe it; but I'm just saying that I find the situation quite confusing at times. And I know that there are people within that government that have worked with the Schiller Institute, that are very familiar with your ideas, and that is largely why Greece is where it is now. But I suppose I'm asking for a kind of update on the Greek situation, if you could just share that with us?

LaRouche: Okay, the answer essentially is that the Greek situation, as such, is in process. Now the prob-

lem is, to come to a final decision on this matter of the Greek thing, consider the fact that it rests on two things. First of all, Europe. Europe is in a state of breakdown—even Germany is at the threat of a breakdown. Other nations are on the edge of a breakdown. We are also on the edge of a war, a general war which is launched by the British Empire, and is potentially prepared, and would be launched by the President of the United States, Obama. That's the situation first.

Now the action of these four Senators, and those who will follow in augmentation of their action, is going to also change the economy. First of all, we're going to eliminate—if they do their job, and I think they will—we are going to eliminate Wall Street. We are going to shut it down. How do we do that? Glass-Steagall. The restitution of the existence of the Glass-Steagall law of Franklin Roosevelt will be a sufficient instrument to protect, now, the United States as it was before. So therefore, what we have to do is go back to the Franklin Roosevelt conception of the principles of reform, which he introduced against bad predecessors, at his time, and actually restore the nature of the intention on Glass-Steagall, which was established initially by President Franklin Roosevelt. That's the solution.

Now in the process, this means that Wall Street, as we know it, is going to disappear. But the point is, you don't simply dump Wall Street; you have to have a program which admits that Wall Street is essentially hopelessly dead. You don't want to leave the corpse around. So therefore, I'm not going to tell you what I think we should do about it, because it has to be decided by members of the Congress, for example, the Senate in particular. And there are certain options which the Senate, or the Congress generally, has for dealing with this question of dumping Wall Street. Those decisions have to be made by relevant authorities in the Federal government.

There can be suggestions, recommendations, and so forth, and I will also make such things. But we understand that there is a solution, which is presently available, to save the economy of the United States, by means which require the shutting down of a bankrupt Wall Street system. I'm not in a position to meddle in how the present government of the United States, especially the Congress, is going to handle these problems. But I am in sympathy with the necessity and urgent performance of solutions which I know are feasible. I know the principles of the things that I know of, define a competence to solve this problem. But to solve the problem involves a process of shaping, and reshaping, some of the law of the United States from the top down.

I shall talk about that; I shall refer to that; but I shall not proclaim a solution, as such. Because I know the four Senators, who led this process of trying to save the United States by Glass-Steagall approaches, implicitly. I'm not going to interfere with it, but I support it. And I will say things to support it, and so forth. But I will always admit, that at this point it is the Senate and Congress of the United States, which has the responsibility for executing the departure of Wall Street from the U.S. economy. I will not specify how they should do that.

Q: [Inaudible]

LaRouche: Greece? Well, of course Greece will be a key factor in the international processes, which should be supported in due course by the United States. That is, these kinds of matters in Europe, in particular, must be settled in terms of diplomatic proceedings in the trans-Atlantic community. This goes not only to the Greek question, and things like that in Europe; it also goes to the world, or the best of the world, including China, notably, including Russia, including nations in Europe otherwise, and in other parts of the world. We are going to have to have a process which reorganizes the planet; essentially you have got to eliminate the British Empire, as it stands today.

What is happening already in that direction, is that China, for example—China has committed a great revolution, which not only is for China itself, but is for the world as a whole. And China is the leading nation of the entire world. China is probably the most advanced, in terms of exploration of nearby space. Other parts of the world have not come up to performance on that.

So therefore, we are now at a point where there are certain nations, or groups of nations, like India, as well as China, and some other nations, such as in South America, which have already [adopted] the same thing: It's called the BRICS. And so the BRICS policy, and things like it or related to it, are already implicitly the next step required as we get out of the mess of the world today, including in the United States, including other parts of Europe, and so forth. And China is a very important part of this whole thing. Also, look at certain

EIRNS/Christopher Lewis

The importance of Greece to the nations of the BRICS is reflected in the attention China is paying to Europe, and especially the Balkan region. Here, Chinese Foreign Minister Li Kejiang at the December 2014 meeting of the Forum of China and the Central and Eastern European Countries, held in Belgrade, Serbia.

nations in South America. Look at some ambitious nations, which are not too powerful right now, but in Africa.

So, going on before us we have a general revolution throughout the world, in terms of not only particular nations and their particular problems, but their relationships with others—the changing relationship among nations. You already have something good going on in much of the world, outside of the trans-Atlantic area. But we also need, and we must have, a more general comprehensive view for most parts of the world.

You know, you can always have a dissenting point, here and there, and so forth. That's not a big issue. You can deal with that. But the principal body of the nations of the planet, while they will retain their actual independence, will also at the same time, as China is doing with the "win-win" concept, and what's happening in South America, come together on a joint, common-interest basis, on a global scale.

The British Imperial Enemy

Speed: Let me just read this question from Sean, first. Lyn, Sean Stone is a correspondent now for *RT, Russia Today*, and he was in Athens on Friday, July 3, Saturday the 4th, and then for the vote. He had the following question. He talked about how on Friday there were about 50,000 people in the square. He saw the enthusiasm of the people. But he wondered this: With what he saw coming back, with what happened with the Chinese stock market and the various other things, he said: What's actually going on? Is this a financial Armageddon?

Then the second part of his question is: What exactly should Americans do who understand the importance of what happened in Athens, to make the reintroduction of Glass-Steagall a reality?

LaRouche: Okay. This is complicated, but it's not that complicated. What happened is that the European system, backed by the British Empire, the Queen herself, and circles like Wall Street in the United States, have created a global situation in which the Greeks have been increasingly *raped* by chiefly the British Empire, but also by other nations on the continent of Europe. That's the chief problem. What has happened is, the Greeks have revolted.

Queen Elizabeth and Royal Consort Prince Philip on an October 2008 visit to the Slovak Republic.

Now the Greeks in a state of revolt, have very little in terms of financial resources among the nations of Europe and also beyond. But we do not intend—not only me, but many parts of the world—do not intend to leave the Greeks in the degree of impoverishment which they have been victimized by the British Empire and by the other nations of Europe. That is, they have *raped* Greece!

The way it happened is that some of the Greek governments were intimidated and became opportunist, and sold out Greece, for the sake of their own short-term purposes. In other words, they pledged debts to other nations, and these debts could not be repaid. But the problem was the raping of Greece by its victimization. That is, when the Greeks were not able to fund their own operations, rather than fighting on that issue, they let the Greek population suffer, in the main.

Therefore the question here is, first, how do we get the Greeks back what are their justified powers. Now, they have a government now, and the government is a good one, so far. I will not talk about the indefinite future. But anyway, it's good.

And Greece has allies. Now these are not allies, like war allies in the ordinary sense, but there's an agreement from other nations that *Greece must be defended*, and that there must be a successful form of emergency effort, to bring better order in the Greek situation. Now, for the Greeks themselves and for the Greek nation, that is an urgent issue. It's not something for "down the

line." We're talking about a relatively short period of time. For example, Russia is a main protector of the Greeks. Now, how far Russia will go in the short term, is not knowable. But if everything comes to the worst, Russia is one of the nations which will be very important, for defending Greece, if other parts of the European system don't come across with something good. And I'm sure of that.

And we have members associated with me, who are very much devoted to that, particularly on the Greek question directly, who are working closely in and out with leading Greek figures.

So this is not something to worry about, as a long-term perspective. What we're doing is we're fighting a short-term war. And Schäuble in Germany, Merkel in Germany, are real problems; France is *mezzo-mezzo*, as the Italians would say.

In Britain, Britain is a mixed-up thing. The British monarchy is for genocide. What the policy is right now with the British monarchy, *and* of California, the governor of California, and similar places, is to reduce the population of the planet, from seven billion people to one. And the project is on now. The project is organized by the British Empire, the British Queen, the whole kit and caboodle; they've always had that kind of policy. They've always been for mass murder, for mass reduction of human population, and so forth and so on. That is, the British Royal Family is one of the most evil, most Satanic forces on this planet.

And ultimately the problem the Greeks face, still today, is the effect of the British Empire, in its influence in the nation as a whole. Now, naturally, my inclination is, that nonsense has got to stop. We're going to do something about it. And there are nations such as China,—don't worry about China's problem; there is no big problem. It's being spelled out by the British, especially Wall Street, especially Obama. President Obama is really one of the real problems here. Otherwise, on the China problems: Obama's done that, or it's done on his behalf, underscored.

So we do not have to worry about the Greeks, and say that they're doing something terrible, or that China's collapsing—nonsense! Absolute nonsense! *Greece will not be abandoned!* It will not be abandoned. We're going to have to do something rough on that.

Remember, right now, something very good is happening: Four Senators of the United States have taken steps to defend the *United States* itself, against the onrushing collapse of Wall Street! So, we're in a period of possibilities for great change, if we don't make a mess of our options. And that's the way to look at these things.

Glass-Steagall Is In Process

Q: Thank you very much, my name is R—. I have a question: How does the passage of Glass-Steagall raise people's awareness via Classical music?

LaRouche: The problem in respect to Classical music, is something which Wall Street has actually been chiefly responsible for. I mean, all the idiots running around, playing we don't know what; they're playing something and they're making noises. We're not quite sure what the root of the thing is.

But you have to look at this fact. There's a dividing line in modern history, in the European and so forth part of the world. What happened is, in the beginning of the Twentieth century, with people like [David] Hilbert and Bertrand Russell, successfully introduced a process of destruction of the systemic intellectual, and related characteristics of the U.S. population.

This coincided with the ouster of [Chancellor Otto von] Bismarck from his office in Germany. Bismarck had been a very close ally, but indirectly, cautiously shall we say,—but he was supporting Abraham Lincoln in the Civil War; that is, not the war itself, but to support Lincoln and what he represented. And Bismarck's economic policies during that period, and the period since Lincoln's assassination, were dedicated to a new economic order in the world. But what happened is, that period leading into the Twentieth Century, was a period of mass murders: The President of France, assassinated; other Presidents of other nations, assassinated; bloody wars in various spots exploded, during that period of the last ten years of the Nineteenth Century.

So there was a change in things, in the direction of decadence, from which the United States has never been freed. Franklin Roosevelt, of course, was excellent. Other people who followed him, like Kennedy, excellent! Ronald Reagan, excellent, though he had a Vice President who was a real bad piece of work. These are the realities that we deal with.

Now we're at the point where Wall Street is absolutely bankrupt. It may maintain some fragment of its financial interest, but right now it's on the edge; it's on the edge of a complete collapse, and I welcome such a collapse. I welcome the collapse on the condition that something else, good, is in there to fix the problem.

I think what the four Senators have done, in restoring the appeal for Glass-Steagall, is the action which is required. And I think at this point, as a matter of practice—there are many other things I could say about this—I would say the fact that Glass-Steagall is now on the agenda, inside the United States, through the Senate, and since Wall Street is in very, very deep problems—it's bankrupt in fact—whether it's able to wiggle or not is another matter; but more or less inevitably, Wall Street is finished! If it's not finished, then the planet's finished, more or less.

I think we're going to win. But we have to understand the processes: Don't rely upon events as such. Because events are always in process. The question is, what is the process doing? In what direction is the process going? Or what are the factors which determine how the process will go? And I welcome very richly, the idea of the removal of anything opposed to Glass-Steagall. I hate Wall Street. I hate 'em because I'm smart enough to know that I should hate them.

Let's not worry too much about these things. But look at what is in process; always look at what's in process. What's the direction? What's the motion? What are the factors that people are going to revolt against? For example, the O'Malley case: O'Malley is not featured, officially, as being a probable President of the United States now. But he's looking closer and closer in that direction. Why? Because the other guys are no good! Like the Bushes! Who would want to vote for a Bush? Moses should burn all the Bushes!

We've got to have a realistic idea, not a so-called "simple fact" explanation. The world is in flux; the world has *always* been in flux, more or less, at least in civilized times. So we are now in a process. My function, like your function, should be how to change the course of events, in order to solve the problems which confront mankind, both in the United States, and among nations generally.

Q: [starts mid-sentence] ... a problem that maybe you could help me with. I'm very active politically. I go to the Tea Party meetings and such, and all these arguments, as you've been saying, boil down to not the argument; what it really boils down to, is the destruc-tion, the killing, of 85% of the world's human population. And when I bring this up, they look at me like I'm from Venus or outer space. And I don't know how to break this barrier.

The only thing that I can think is that the evil is so diabolical that the goodness within their soul refuses to allow them to face it. Because that's what I get—oh, they make up excuses why it is totally irrational.

I'd like to get from you a hint, so to speak, of how to approach this problem.

LaRouche: We should be approaching it anyway. I've spent most of my life, you know, I've had some experience in economy and things related to that; I've been successful in economics, in financial economics and so forth. And many other things; I've been an effi-cient agent of action in many nations; my wife, of course, has been in China. I was on the edge of China, I never got in there, myself. But that was just coinciden-tal. Indochina, other parts, India—I have a big history in India. Lots of history in Europe. I have lots of history in our economy and in our Presidency. I served briefly under President Reagan, except the Bushes got in the way; the Bushes should have been burned.

But anyway, this is not an impossible situation; we're in flux. We have a battle on our hands. We have no winning position. Take Glass-Steagall: Suddenly, recently, just recently, one Senator called upon three other Senators to activate, not just to introduce but to activate Glass-Steagall. This coincided with the fact

CC/Gregory Hauenstein
Presidential candidate Martin O'Malley, a prominent promoter of Glass-Steagall, greets patrons of Uncle Nancy's Coffeehouse in Newton, Iowa.

that Wall Street was on the verge of a general break-down crisis: Wall Street is no more! It's just a matter of burying the corpse.

And the only thing that's holding up the death of Wall Street, as an institution, is the fact of going through the formalities of creating its successor, and that, as I said earlier here today, that's a question on which au-thorities of the United States government, the Con-gress, the Senate and the Congress generally, and other institutions, must make a decision. I will be imploring, shall we say, things that I already agree with what they're doing, with what they've done, the four Sena-tors. They did the right thing! They have taken actions which lead to the possibility of defending the existence of the United States, against what the Wall Street col-lapse could do! They know things, they have the intel-ligence to understand this; they have the sources of in-telligence to know what to do. It just takes the guts to do it. And I think these four Senators have shown a sign of the guts to do it.

O'Malley, for example. I don't know if I want him to be the next President of the United States; I certainly would prefer him, far, far, far above anything like Obama! But I think he's a good potential candidate. In my view, he, with his policies already, is potentially a suitable candidate to replace and dump Obama; and that would be a very, very good thing.

Those kinds of things have to happen. But the prob-lem is, we're now at a point where I think we have everything in our hands in the United States among appropriate leading circles, including leading circles of the highest level of Congress: I think we can do the job. My concern is to support those people who are going to do the job; and also to recognize that it is *they*, not me, who have the authority to choose and shape the way we're going to get rid of the bums, the rascals. And how we're going to solve the problem for the coming period of time for the solution to this crisis.

Our Internal Enemy

Q: Hi, Mr. LaRouche; my name is R—. It's an honor to speak with you; I've been following you for twenty years and plus, since I was in law school. My question relates to the IMF and NATO and the British Empire. Obviously, from a realistic standpoint, the United States has inherited the mantle of the British Empire; or at least certain forces in the United States have inherited the British Empire from my understanding. And that NATO is sort of the military arm; whereas the IMF/World Bank is the financial arm of the British Empire. And it seems like we're on a collision course, as you said earlier, with the rest of the world, in a sense.

How do we integrate the United States of America—which really should believe in the spirit of free competition according to the Sherman Act even—how do we integrate the U.S. into the BRICS paradigm in a way that's voluntary?

LaRouche: OK; we have one problem in answer to that question. One big problem. It's the loss of Glass-Steagall, and the Obama Administration and the Bush Administration that preceded Obama. These are the chief obstacles, not some foreign obstacle; no. It's inside the United States.

Now, of course, Obama is an agent of the British monarchy; that's how he got his job. The same way that Schwarzenegger got his job in California. Remember, he was the whore-master of Europe in his earlier proceedings, and the British system pulled him into California; and then inserted him into a different role, as a movie star. Then they made him a governor,—and what he did, destroyed the government of California. I mean, the original Governor of California [Pat Brown] was a good man; his son, who's now in charge, is an absolute idiot, and a very not-nice person—on the contrary.

So, we have these kinds of problems, but the problems come from disasters which were large-scale economic disasters which are caused by bad policy. The cancellation of Glass-Steagall was actually a treason against the United States, in fact. It may not be recognized as such, but to anyone who is looking at it from an economic standpoint or a scientific standpoint, that was a crime against the United States.

And it happened because Bill Clinton was set up; that's how it happened. It was set up by the British monarchy, the Queen herself gave the orders; and the Republican Party team carried it out. They knocked Bill Clinton out.

Now remember, in this case, I was actually working in Russia; I was invited to come to visit there; because they wanted my expert advice on what to do about their economic crisis. So, they invited me to Moscow to hear their description of the situation, and to ask my expert advice on economy. We came up with a proposal which I said "yes" to, and they agreed; and we aimed that proposal to a delivery of negotiations with Russia, based on the openings being created by President Bill Clinton.

What happened to Bill Clinton, to get a clear idea of how these things go, Bill Clinton did not act immediately on my recommendation. He was sympathetic to it. This was a funny relationship, because Bill and I never had a direct connection; we had very good indirect connections. As a matter of fact, he saved my life among other things; that's a pretty good connection.

So this financial problem today is of that nature; it comes into that category. And if we in the United States get rid of Obama, before he can lead us into a thermonuclear war; that is, a thermonuclear extermination war, which is possible during this summer of this year unless we get that bum out of there; or get somebody else to bump him out of there. Expel him from office! He's a criminal, he's committed crimes, great crimes. His Administration has done great crimes; even greater than the crimes of Cheney and the dumb Bushes.

Our problem is *that*! We don't control our own nation, because Wall Street's ties with certain elements in the United States use money, chiefly, money control, swindles, in order to control the United States. And from all the things I've known, the United States has been [under that control], since Bill Clinton actually left office. He was being booted out already, and he gave up on Glass-Steagall. Just before he left office, he dumped Glass-Steagall, and that caused the great Wall Street boom. And then Britain, which has ruined the United States since that time.

But now we have a Congress that's recognized that Wall Street has to be dumped, and that means it has to be done. It has to be done now. And now we have four Senators, leading Senators, who have pushed the Glass-Steagall reform. Once you get the Glass-Steagall reform in place in the United States now, you're going to find a big, big change for the better. Now the change will be something like what Franklin Roosevelt meant when he became President. He made radical changes, but they were the right changes; proper, moral changes, in accord with our Constitution. All we need now, if we can prevent war from happening, is to retread the tracks of Franklin Roosevelt's election, and what he did in the first period of his term as President is the same principle of action which he represented throughout the entirety of his own Presidency. That's what you can count on.

White House/Pete Souza

President Obama discusses his confrontation policy toward Russia with Ukrainian President Petro Poroshenko in Washington, Sept. 18, 2014.

Q: Hello, Mr. LaRouche; this is J——. My question is: Recently, the dreaded secret TPP—Trans-Pacific Partnership—was approved by the entire Congress of cowards and sycophants. These traitors in Congress cannot be persuaded by the citizens alone; we must pressure our local state and local reps to persuade the House of Representatives to impeach Obama—even though they are cowards. And both chambers to reinstate Glass-Steagall.

LaRouche: You can say the intention of doing Glass-Steagall now, is a pretty solid blow in motion. We have one Senator who signalled to the other three, "We've got to get the Glass-Steagall thing into motion now."

Now, the relevant action now; don't look at fixed positions. Always look at the process of change, and see which direction of change you want to go in and how well you can do it, if you want to do it.

Right now, if Obama were to be continued in office, then I'd say, because he's an agent of the British Empire, and the British Empire has a longstanding policy, to reduce the population of the planet Earth from seven billion people to less than one billion people. That's the intention; that's the intention which motivates Obama—that's what he is. Look at his health care policies; look at his practices. This man is, by instinct, a murderer. Look, he's an assassin! No President has a right to go out there and assassinate people, the way he did it. Maybe the target's a criminal, but you have to follow some discretion in terms of fair justice; and we don't have it. And you have also under the Cheney Administration, you had some of the same kinds of stuff.

Now, we've come to a point where the leading people, the smart people, the conscious-stricken people in the United States, and those with some knowledge and influence, have to come to the point of saying: "Wall Street? Forget it! Dump it!" Build a new organization based on the precedent of Glass-Steagall, which is what the Senate has done. That would eliminate already most of the economic evils; some of the things that we have from one candidate for President is also very useful. I know these things very well.

The time has come for certain changes to be made immediately, or relatively immediately; but also, what one has to change immediately is the attitude that most American citizens feel—a feeling of impotence. Now, feeling that you're impotent, is like getting cowardly in the period of battle. And what we need are people who are determined, but with decision and with competence to make presentations as the four Senators have done on the Glass-Steagall initiative. Now, what they've done, if carried through, will save the nation. And that's why I think you need to look at it that way. We have to march along the road which leads to victory; don't stand still, move, advance along the road to victory.

Speed:: While the next questioner is coming up, I just want to say that you reminded me, when you said that, Lyn, of Sylvia Lee; who had a spiritual she used to do—actually an anthem—called "March on, and you shall see the victory. March on, and you shall see the day."

LaRouche: Yes, yes, yes. That was delightful. She was a wonderful woman.

Obama's Extermination Agenda

Q: Good afternoon, my name is C—. I have only two questions. They appear broad, but they really hit the spot of Wall Street's business. One question is, what will the government's perspective be if Wall Street disappears, in terms of these programs for the people in need, especially in the City of New York?

Because I like pro-activity, and sometimes, the government gets involved in too much rhetoric, too much talking, and no action. So I would like to know what they're going to do. Because Wall Street is going to fall of its own weight. You don't have to be a psychic. But I would like to know what the government is going to do?

Among the early victims of the genocide policy being imposed in California are the farm workers, like the one shown here.

The second question is, what is the International Monetary Fund going to do with Greece and Puerto Rico? Because they have to do something. This time it's not a question of analyzing, thinking about it, putting it off for tomorrow; they have to do something or otherwise, the United States is going to pay a big price for not being a leader, and being a follower of the British Empire.

LaRouche: Well, this problem is really on the edge of solution, because you do have right now an intention by the United States Senate, by the leaders of the Senate, and by the implicit intention of many other Americans,—the fact is, Wall Street is already broken down; it has reached a limit beyond which it cannot extend its expectations. The United States economy,—the extinction is likely, under those conditions.

But now the point is, that now that the Glass-Steagall resolution has been re-introduced into Congress, the reactions and effects of that mean that this is not a frozen situation. Yes, you're right in saying that these things have happened; you're right in saying that nothing much has been done about the injustice. Well, of course, that's true.

That has been the case of the Twentieth Century. Since the beginning of the Twentieth Century, and of the wars which occurred in the last decade of the Nineteenth Century, there's been a general trend of decadence and degeneration among nations both in Europe and the United States, and around the nations which surround the United States. This is true, no question about it. It seems like an impossible, permanent disease.

Well, I would say, that's not true. You've got two options right now. If the British Empire and Obama have their way, then the extinction of the human species is a possibility, on short notice, even this summer. Because what the British are doing now, is an intention of mass murder, of reducing the population of the United States and other nations from its present population to less than one. That's what the policy is; down to one billion people at most, is allowed.

Food is going to be destroyed, according to them. Wall Street and the greenies are out to murder the people of the United States. How? Well, the Governor of California is determined to murder the citizens of the United States, by a green policy; which is the same thing as the British policy; which is the same place as the ancient Zeus policy. This is real evil. And unless you can fight that evil, are willing to fight the evil, and understand how to defeat it, we don't have any chance.

But I know we *do* have a chance. And some other people in other parts of the world know it, too. Actually the development of the BRICS motion, while some parts of Central America are not in good shape, has not been supported, this is largely the effect of Obama. I mean the real downturn, came with the entry of Obama into the Presidency!

If you look at what Bill Clinton tried to do on this thing, it's a clear indication. Here's a former President, looking backwards, even though he's been kicked around a little bit, and he recognized what the truth is about this man.

We now have come to a time where the trend of actions, direction of actions, is against the green policy, but against the British policy, against the mass-killing policy throughout Africa and the Middle East; and the nations like Russia, China, India, and somewhat smaller nations, some in South America, are all against this nonsense.

We are now where the United States' power, as an economic power, is out of control. Wall Street is bankrupt! That is clear. Wall Street right now is *totally bankrupt*. It's super-bankrupt! It's been stretched already into bankruptcy, many times over. Now, the prick has come to the balloon. Wall Street is finished. That's the good news!

And all the things you're talking about come to that thing. The point is, the question is not what has happened; the question is what can we *make* happen, and how do we do it? Well, the very fact that four Senators who are designated, for a Glass-Steagall policy and have adopted it; and Wall Street is bankrupt,—what are the leading bankers going to do, therefore? They're bankrupt! Their institutions, their trillions of dollars of assets, that they claim to have both in the United States and beyond, where it's got them to? It's gone! And the only thing is, we've got to do is to step up, take charge, and take the next step. They're finished!

Effective action by the leadership of the Senate is sufficient motive to bring those kinds of evil you referred to [to an end]: Get rid of them; correct the problem. The time has come to win, not to complain, but to win: The chance is now. We have to make it now. [applause]

Speed:: Let me point out, that there are 37 state legislators in New York that endorsed the Glass-Steagall reinstatement resolution that we circulated during the last session. There are three Congresspersons, including Charles Rangel, who have also done so.

And were this meeting—and of course Mr. LaRouche intends to continue this dialogue here in New York,—were this meeting to resolve that it is going to work in the way that it can, on behalf of this, I'm confident we can create a situation both in Manhattan, and more generally in New York State, where the prospects for the passage of Glass-Steagall become more likely because of what we do here.

I should just say that the New York director for the League of United Latin American Citizens introduced at the National Conference of LULAC, a resolution to reinstate Glass-Steagall. I don't know if that group has voted on that today or not, but the point is there's plenty

that we can do. March on, and you will gain the victory. [The resolution carried.— ed.]

Greece Will Be Defended

Q. Hello, LaRouche? It's the first time here. I'm not very familiar with everything, but I'm getting more familiar. First off, I have many, many things that—Oh, my name is John; I'm Greek myself. And there are some things that confuse me.

First of all, I thought that IMF is a Western invention, the United States supported it, and BRICS is an antagonist, it's something opposite. And I'm not sure how Americans can get into BRICS and like BRICS. That's one thing that confuses me a little bit.

Another thing is that Tsipras, the Greek Prime Minister, is a traitor. He is against the Greek Constitution, and he signed the new memorandum where it stated that he cannot get money from other places. That happened yesterday, last night; very late at night.

It was one of the things that the IMF and the Europeans asked him to sign, and, of course, he did, because he was put into power by them, and Mr. Soros was funding his party in Greece. And so, whatever he said before the elections, now he did exactly the opposite.

Now, another thing is that the Greek Revolution was never completed. Once the Greeks got freed, after the American Revolution, was the Greek Revolution. So we had all these other people, all the Greek Presidents, were shipped from the United States to Greece, even Mr. Karamanlis, Mr. Papandreou; you know they were prepared here and they were sent there, even without real elections. Everything was against the Greeks. It was about other people and other nations.

And the last thing is, I heard you talking about Zeus. I want to tell you that the Olympic spirit, which Zeus represents, and the Greek spirit, which is the Olympic spirit, is the spirit which I think everybody at some point should start getting into, in order to be able to make a better humanity, and make a more beautiful world.

Anyway, these are some comments, questions, whatever. And I want to see how you feel about these things. It might sound really crazy or out of place, some of them, anyway, yes. Thank you.

LaRouche: Okay! Well, I would say the first thing we probably should take up, of the points you've just listed, is the question of Zeus. Because the death of Zeus was the beginning of the triumph of Greece. That's a good thing. And you find all over the symbols around Greece, it's loaded with this history. It shows up in various ways.

The Greek port of Piraeus, a key commericial hub for the Maritime Silk Road.

The fact that the Greeks were broken, it was a plan; it was an intention. Look, if you look at the map, and I gather since you're Greek-speaking, you know what the agenda is in terms of the map of Greece. And Greece represented a very important strategic point in the Mediterranean; that's how it was able to function. First of all, it's commerce; it's many other things. Even when parts of Greece degenerated, the tradition of Greece, which the Greeks themselves had lost at that point in a degeneration, but Nicholas of Cusa, and others, stepped in—Nicholas of Cusa personally, this great leader of Christianity, stepped in, and adopted the Greek tradition as a working device, for the development of the new system, the Renaissance, the great Renaissance.

And so, now we're in a point where everybody is, in tradition, in the tradition of Greece; for example, also because the temple was there, still, when Nicholas of Cusa went there. That is the tradition: That's the tradition of Christianity; it's the tradition of many other things, essentially.

Therefore, the Greeks will not be abandoned by the Creator; we can be assured of that. They have suffered, but on top of that, the Greeks, if we have anything to say about it, are not going to continue to suffer. Not only because we are a great, giving people—that's not the point; we need the Greeks! They're a factor which we need, their skills; and we want them to come back, into a position of strength. It's economic strength, social strength. They're a fighting people, anyway, and we're seeing that now: They're fighting very courageously. And some of

us, including some people in Germany, believe it or not,—some big thieves in Germany don't like that, but I do, and others do.

Now Greece is being defended. The problem is, how do we negotiate the process of that defense? We try to deal with things at different levels. In other words, you've tried to chew down on the opposition position, which is largely the European system; the European system as it is now. The European system has been and remains, the source of the suffering of the Greek people; and the continuation of that suffering. So therefore, we have to look at it from that standpoint.

We have to get a victory, for Europe itself, as well as the United States, and that will not be a victory, unless Greece also has its rightful position. Because Greece is very much needed by us; if you just look at the map, the map of history, since Zeus was crushed. The death of Zeus was the best thing that ever happened for Greece. And that's the tradition; we have to fix it. And fixing it, is something I absolutely advocate; we're not going to shirk it, we're going to fix it.

The Hamilton Principle

Q: Good afternoon, everyone. I'm B—, I'm here from the U.S. Virgin Islands, St. Croix. We're here in New York, and you may not be aware that there was a terrible murder today committed. It affected the United States. Now, fortunately, it happened 211 years ago: Alexander Hamilton was shot today. So I just wanted to report that local news to you.

But, on a larger issue, I agree with some of the things you say, but certainly not all. I spent many years in office when I was in my thirties; I was a mayor of a city of 100,000 here in the U.S., though I've lived in the Virgin Islands now for many, many, many decades, for most of my adult life. And I can say something: The United States Virgin Islands has double the personal debt of Puerto Rico, which has double the personal debt of Greece.

But here's my question, too: In my experience, and

I'm politically involved in the islands, the demand for debt comes from below, not above. The demand for debt comes from government [inaud]ible unions, people working for the government, people demanding that the government spend money often on themselves. Now, there's obviously some legitimacy in that, but when you're not building roads, and you're not building bridges, and you're not using the money for those hard things—you know, I'm an architect, so I think in those terms—but when you're not using the money for those long-term things, the debt becomes a very difficult and dangerous proposition for many countries and little territories, like the Virgin Islands.

How do you feel about the demand for government spending coming from *below*, not from above?

LaRouche: Let's say very simply, you just have to follow the principles of Alexander Hamilton. That's the short answer. And if you know the real history of his role, while he lived. And including the fact that some of the leading colonies which brought together his enemies, and that they were evil people, that certain Presidents of the United States who were successors to Alexander Hamilton's role; the people who assassinated him, and the people who hated him, apart from those who assassinated him, directly, the problem has been *treason* in the United States, performed largely as treason by the Southern states of the United States. The ones that lived on racism, that's what the problem is.

What happens is, in these island areas you referred to, what's the effort? It's the same thing. It doesn't have a black skin, it has a brown skin, or a light skin; same thing. It's a category of people, who have, since the Roman Empire—the Roman Empire!—have made practices, and mass-murderous practices, and the Roman Empire was purely evil, like the British Empire today, which is *purely evil*. Now that doesn't mean that every Briton is evil, but it means the British oligarchy is!

EIRNS/Stuart Lewis
Alexander Hamilton's statue in Manhattan.

Every oligarch, very, very evil! It's the most evil thing on the planet! And Obama works for it.

That's the question! How do you get rid of Obama, in time to save civilization? How do you get rid of Wall Street, in time to save civilization and the people of the United States? How do you eliminate the racist characters, which still permeate the Southern states of the United States? What do you say about the fact that Florida has the highest rate of homicide of any state in the nation? *These* are the realities, not "facts" as such, treated in abstract, but the process of history. What are the forces which deal with the process of history? Motion! Not fixed things, not complaints about fixed problems. How do you change things, move them, so that the things that should have been removed, *are* removed?

Remember, the third President of the United States, was a raving idiot! a murderous idiot! Who hated Alexander Hamilton and who did much to destroy the first Presidencies of the United States; who was behind the assassination of Alexander Hamilton, and so forth and so on? *These* are the issues. The issue lies not in the event, but in the history of the process of the event. And that's something I've learned very richly, through most of my life, and remember, I'm a 90-year-old observer.

Obama Must Be Removed

Q: Peace, Brother LaRouche. My name is C——, I'm from Brooklyn. I'm on a little different subject, but it's still the same crisis. Have you heard about Jade Helm 15? A military exercise that will be held in 9 to 15 states in the U.S.A. between July 15 and September 15th, Florida and New York are included.

What concerns me is that due to the fact that it's the military—in New York they say it's the police and the National Guard; but due to the fact that it's the military, false flags can go, and martial law can be called any time this summer.

LaRouche: Yeah. True. That's a fact. I understand the fact in terms that I've warned, as I said—and I've been following this and I'm an expert in it—that Obama has been long intending, because he's a British agent; that's how he got to be President; the process is known. And you know the first successful election that he had for President, was based on British orders, British backing. It's the British Kingdom, the British monarchy who put Obama into power.

Now, they left some skunks there beforehand, Cheney: Cheney's one of the nastiest, most evil persons I know of in the United States. He still is. And Obama is the same thing. He's a stooge. He's not the top man, but he has a top man in the case of the British monarchy, which will kick him around and make sure he does what the Queen wants. That's the way he functions. That's how he got to be President of the United States: It was the British Empire, and I know the facts of the matter, who put him in power. So he should never have been in power. He should be removed.

So what's happening now? Obama is the agent, under British direction, the British Queen's direction, to launch a general thermonuclear war, throughout much of the planet, and the danger is coming up now, in these months. I don't know what date it will occur in, but I know we better get him out of there, *fast*, and get the Congress to do something about throwing him out of office. It's an impeachment. We've done that before. This man must be impeached, because the powers that the British Empire expresses through him, as their agent, is the greatest threat to humanity and to the United States itself.

So therefore, this guy should be removed. Now, the pressures that are happening now may cause his removal anyway. But the danger is,— and I know this man very well—this agent Obama, I know him very, very well; it doesn't take much to know him, once you understand what the rules of the game are. But this man is evil, *purely evil*. But he's only an agent of the British Queen. And the policy of the British Queen, is—and has been before—to reduce the human population of the planet Earth, to *less than 1 billion people, now!* Not in the distant future, now! Immediately!

And they've taken over a Pope; the current Pope is a supporter of the genocide policy of the British Queen. All right, fine: That's the evil that's going on. That's the problem!

But the answer lies, not in a fixed state of affairs. The problem lies in the motion: who is creating the motion that leads in the necessary direction? And I'm confident that I'm supporting that motion. But I'm also celebrating, with some pleasure, the fact that there's some members of our government who understand that something has to be done about all this stuff, right now; including those military officers in the United States service, still, who recognize that we're threatened by the United States being pushed, by Obama, by President Barack Obama, into a war, which would exterminate almost everybody. So we'll have to do something about that: Get him out of office, quick.

The Role of Experienced Teachers

Q: Good afternoon, Mr. LaRouche. This is J—. I'm from Brooklyn, New York. I wanted to talk a little about Glass-Steagall and I know we've gone over this a lot. But as a delegate to the United Federation of Teachers, myself and other colleagues got through a resolution, got a resolution passed through the UFT *and* the AFT, to support Glass-Steagall. It took a lot. Now, we're at a stage where I have written a letter to the delegates; I have to kind of tweak that letter and rewrite it, do some things and present it to those delegates. There are over 200 organizations like the UFT; other unions and other organizations, community organizations, that many of us belong to.

Now, my question is, how can we use the prior work that we've done, the things that we've set up already, to get a breakthrough right now?

LaRouche: Okay! I think there are some other things we have to do that're supplementary to that to make it work. In other words, the idea itself is excellent; the question is, how do we make it work. We have to take up several things: First of all, the fact that Glass-Steagall is being pushed, again, seriously from the Senate. We don't know how durable that motion by the four Senators is, and other people involved as well; but we know that it is a motion which is credible; it's a real action for emergency, relatively immediate action, by the government of the United States, by the Senate of the United States, which is a primary administration of the United States. So that's there.

We also know that the problem has been, and this is a deeper question; I think what you said so far in your remarks, is perfect—I agree with this, there's no difference whatsoever in the urgency of this motion and the accomplishment of steps in that direction are absolutely indispensable.

For example, let's take the case of the New York

teachers union: New York teachers union, the senior members of the New York teachers union, live in a domain which is far above the level of education allowed in New York City, even New York City, in recent times. The reason we have great teachers, who are left in the school systems, is because they're old enough to have survived the practice of teaching, and were shrewd enough to know how to defend the principle of teaching, even under very difficult circumstances; just like some trade unionists and so forth were very serious, and devoted, like some of the leading trade unionists are devoted to science. But they only are encumbered by blocks, and things like that. The same thing here.

The question is, what's the issue? What makes the difference? Well, the problem is again, that since the beginning of the Twentieth Century; this actually began, really in the 1890s; in the Twentieth Century, there was the beginning of general warfare. This coincided essentially with Bismarck's departure from office, because he'd been a great leader. He was the one who created the whole German economic machine-tool industry development. And so that was removed.

That led into a war, a great war. And that great war, which is the Twentieth Century war, long-term, now goes into this century, the new century; and what you see in the schools, as you teachers know, whether you were too young to be born or not, from the period of 1890s to the present time, is a steady degeneration in the teaching, the education of the minds of students, at all levels of educational development.

And this degeneration, for example, at the end of Franklin Roosevelt's life, BOOM! A degeneration, a whole degeneration; which we got some bounce-back from, from a couple of good Presidents, but we then went down again, with the wars fought against the United States, that is, the interests of the United States. We degenerated, again, and again, and again.

Now, look at the educational process and experienced teachers, whether they were as old as I am, or older, or not, know something about this: The process of education, as defined by public institutions of education, even including universities' practices, has been degenerating. And together with that, we have the degeneration of the quality of labor, a degeneration which

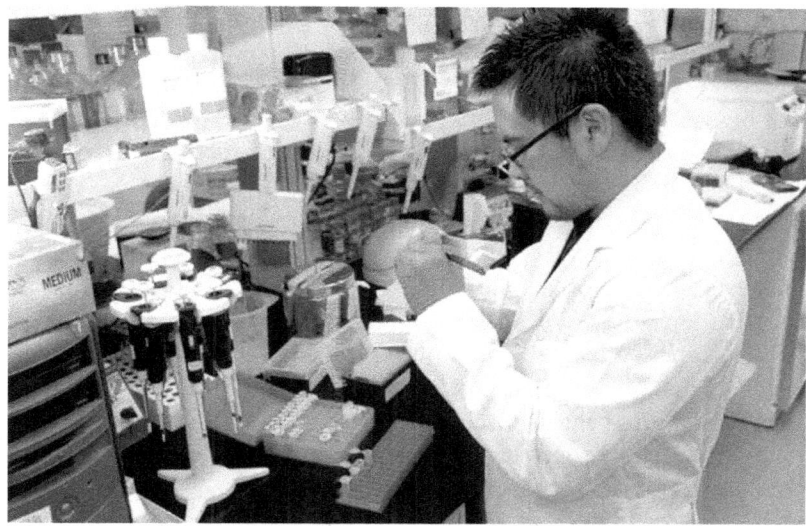

National Institutes of Health

Scientific work like that of this medical laboratory scientist is under threat, due to the degeneration of education in the United States.

activated and associated with, the degeneration of the standard of living, of the quality of skills of the development of the mental powers of the individual, all of this degeneration.

So that therefore, from your nexus, and your age group, of where you have been in New York area, a leading teacher among leading teachers in New York, senior teachers but still living, find out that you're living under New York City which is fairly good in general ways, in education; you see that in the population of the New York City, the families in New York City, which maintain a standard of culture which is high relative to the nation as a whole. But the problem is that the prospect of the coming generation of young people, children and young people, and even middle age people, are actually driven down, in their efficiency and ability to sustain progress in humanity's existence: That's the fight.

And that is the best way to look at this thing. Because look, we all die. We all die, and *will* die, or otherwise. So what is the meaning of life, even for a teacher, *as* a teacher? What's the meaning of life? It's the meaning of what mankind, that now lives, has the ability and willingness, to make discoveries in nature, physical science, and in the general improvement of the preconditions of a better life; the idea that mankind as a continued existence, has a purpose, whereas no animal species as such, has such a purpose, such an immortal purpose. Only mankind has the possibility of that achievement of immortal purpose. That's the most precious thing on the planet.

And the educational process, as in the state of New York school system at its peak, is an example of that—go better, go higher, go better! Look, right now, one of the big issues that I'm dealing with, my associates, for example, is not Glass-Steagall: It's the galactic process. The fact, for example, that the water supply, of life on Earth, is largely dependent upon the superior supply, of water by the Galaxy. Now, what we're doing now in modern science, of people who are intelligent about modern science, we're working on the question of how the Galactic System, in which the Earth system is enclosed, how this system changes the options which man achieves, through man's discovery in the nature of scientific discoveries' progress. And that's what the issue is.

The issue is to recognize, we are not copycats. One baby and adult, and another baby—it's not the same thing. Human beings are not properly copycats. The human species is properly destined to achieve things that earlier generations of humanity have never achieved! And these were not just rewards, these were achievements of mankind. *Mankind becomes a more powerful influence in the universe, within the Galaxy now.* And the idea of breeding children, and breeding people, is progress in the power of mankind to achieve a destined future higher order of existence, for reasons and purposes, which we now *begin* or can begin, to understand of the true nature of mankind.

Mankind is an immortal species, as no animal species otherwise can be!

Hamilton Against Slavery

Speed:: All right. I wanted to say something before you give a summary, and I just do this partially because, as was said by the previous questioner, this is a day of infamy; but at the same time, there's an Alexander Hamilton that people should know about.

The project that Alexander Hamilton created as a secret project with John Jay, and with his friend, Col. John Laurens who was the son of the head of the Continental Congress, and I will read you what that project was, this by way of asking a question for someone in the audience, who isn't coming to the podium, but was asking about South Carolina.

So this is Alexander Hamilton to John Jay; this is Alexander Hamilton, 1779, at the age of 24. And he says this: [as written]

Col Laurens, who will have the honor of delivering you this letter, is on his way to South Caro-

lina, on a project, which I think, in the present situation of affairs there, is a very good one and deserves every kind of support and encouragement. This is to raise two three or four batalions [sic] of [slaves]; with the assistance of the government of that state [South Carolina], by contributions from the [slave] owners in proportion to the number they possess. If you should think proper to enter upon the subject with him, he will give you a detail of his plan. He wishes to have it recommended by Congress to the state [of South Carolina]; and, as an inducement, that they would engage to take those batalions into Continental pay.

It appears to me, that an expedient of this kind, in the present state of Southern affairs, is the most rational, that can be adopted, and promises very important advantages. Indeed, I hardly see how a sufficient force can be collected in that quarter without it. . . .

I foresee that this project will have to combat much opposition from prejudice and self-interest. The contempt we have been taught to entertain for the blacks, makes us fancy many things that are founded neither in reason nor experience; and an unwillingness to part with property of so valuable a kind will furnish a thousand arguments to show the impracticability or pernicious tendency of a scheme which requires such a [financial] sacrifice. But it should be considered, that if we do not make use of them in this way, the enemy probably will; and that the best way to counteract the temptations ... will be to offer them ourselves. *An essential part of the plan is to give them their freedom with their muskets.* This will secure their fidelity, animate their courage, and I believe will have a good influence upon those who remain, by opening a door to their emancipation. . . . [emphasis added by Speed]

So, 235 years ago, Alexander Hamilton, John Laurens, and John Jay were involved in a conspiracy to equip slaves with weapons, and emancipate them. This is important, because we have argued, and Mr. LaRouche in particular has argued, that the Alexander Hamilton that *he* knows, which may not be the Alexander Hamilton that *you* know, is the moral template for us in Manhattan and us in New York to understand and to emulate; not merely because of his work on econom-

wikipedia commons

This New York African Free School has its origins in the New York Manumission Society established by Alexander Hamilton and John Jay (among others), back in the 1780s. This is a lithograph of the second school, done in 1922, after an 1830 engraving from a drawing by student Patrick H. Reason.

ics, but because of *this*, this moral position and opposition to slavery.

And so I just wanted to say that, Lyn, because as you probably know, yesterday, in South Carolina, the Confederate flag was lowered to great cheering among thousands of people who were there; this being done directly in response to the killings that had occurred, and the fact that the family members, when they confronted the killer, said to the killer that they forgave him. And this created such shame, and such a sense of elevation on a certain level, that that Confederate flag no longer flies in South Carolina. [applause]

So I wanted to segue to you and your summary to us as to what we need to do, any other remarks you'd like to give us, as we close out this portion of our dialogue.

LaRouche: Well, the unfortunate part about that story, which is a true story, is the fact of a leading figure [Thomas Jefferson] who was an opponent of this policy, who was a leading opponent of the whole thing, of the mission. And when Hamilton was assassinated, then that man who was the slave-owner, from the state of Virginia, created what became the *evil* of the Southern states, the murderous evil of the Southern states. That's what the issue was.

There is no honor in that stuff. Yeah, people were trying have the slaves become freed, with ammunition and weapons to boot; that was not an idle talk. That's what Alexander Hamilton intended. Alexander Hamil-

ton was the longstanding enemy of Thomas Jefferson, who was the third President of the United States. And the Presidents which immediately followed him, were also stooges of that nature.

And then finally there was another President [John Quincy Adams] who came in. He created the 48 states of the United States in his one term, and then he was kicked out of office, by a Southern evil character [Andrew Jackson], a madman, a complete degenerate of every degree! An Indian killer! All kinds of cruel things: And he was the President for two terms, followed by his successors and their successors. And most of the Presidents of the United States after that thing, up until Lincoln, were evil! There were a couple of good ones, or decent ones shown.

And you had Abraham Lincoln, and you had a great general [Grant], who set up two terms as President of the United States; and we had another President [McKinley] who was a genius—and he, too, was assassinated, to bring to two terms of a bastard [Teddy Roosevelt] into place.

And most of the Presidents were evil. Most of the history of the United States, most of the Presidents were more or less evil. There were some significant exceptions; I served, briefly, under one of those Presidents, Reagan. And we ran a great operation together for several years on his ticket.

But most of this has been—the Bushes. Once the Bush family got into the business of the Presidency, the Bushes are nothing! Prescott Bush was an *evil man*, a purely evil man! He practically invented Nazism; and the Bush family has maintained that tradition,—except most of the Bushes who were his successors turned out to be stupid. And therefore, they are nasty, and dangerous, but they're not intelligent. Cheney is probably a real evil bastard, who would fit that requirement; but he didn't get to be the President. Obama is evil, and he is President. We've got to fix that.

Speed:: Okay, do you have anything else?

LaRouche: If there's anything they want to hear, yes; I'm full of things I'd like to say, but I think I don't occupy an indefinite amount of space! I'm still going to be alive—I think so, unless somebody kills me. I have a certain degree of relative longevity, and I intend to make the most of it.

Speed:: So, I want everybody to join me in thanking Lyn, and he'll be here with us again next week. [applause]

LaRouche: Absolutely!

The Murder of Greece

July 14—Upon reflection on the new and brutal cruelties just imposed on the Greek nation and people by European "leaders," Lyndon La-Rouche declared last evening,

> This is a genocide, which is being steered from Britain, and it is the death knell of the European Union.
>
> The EU will disintegrate. It is the British Empire which has done this. They operated through the German Finance Minister, Schäuble, who represents the extreme right-wing influence on German Chancellor Merkel. But Germany cannot get by with this. Therefore, it, too, now will go into a crisis.
>
> And more than that, this British-driven breakdown crisis of the European Union, also represents a serious and immediate danger of war with Russia, and one of fascism.

The day also saw the thorough exposure of Hillary Clinton's disqualifications as a Presidential candidate, by the simple five-word question demanded of her by LaRouche PAC representative Daniel Burke at her New York City speech: "Will you restore Glass-Steagall?"

Her failure to answer, and then her advisor's statement to the press that she will oppose Glass-Steagall, became growing news all over the United States and in the British press.

Responding to this development, LaRouche stated:

> Hillary's political career was a mistake. She's a lawyer, not a scientist. She was asked a question, and refused to tell the truth about it in public. That will kill her.
>
> Her career is now based on supporting Obama—both in her refusing comment, and then in her consultant opposing it. Both reflect the fact that she's still with Obama.
>
> This means that she's exposed as a fake. She has no Glass-Steagall policy, when members of the Senate, do have one. She's implicitly finished in political life, and that, through her own fault. She blew her career, by acting like a dummy opportunist.

The two matters are directly linked, as La-Rouche PAC's Burke made clear in his interviews with press: The euro debt breakdown can trigger a trans-Atlantic banking crisis at any time, and the only sure action against that is to restore Glass-Steagall to force, fast, in the United States in order to push it through in Europe. That is why Senators moved on Glass-Steagall legislation this week, knowing the rapidly growing danger of a new and greater financial crash.